The Vanishing Forest

The Vanishing Forest

The Human Consequences of Deforestation

A Report for the Independent Commission on International Humanitarian Issues

Zed Books Ltd
London and New Jersey

This report does not necessarily reflect the views, individually or collectively, of the members of the Independent Commission on International Humanitarian Issues (ICIHI). It is based on research carried out for ICIHI and was prepared under the supervision of its Secretariat with the guidance of the ICIHI Working Group on Disasters.

The Vanishing Forest was first published by Zed Books Ltd., 57 Caledonian Road, London N1 9BU and 171 First Avenue, Atlantic Highlands, New Jersey 07716, in 1986.

Cover design by Henry Iles
Cover photograph: Land cleared for new highway, Brazil.
Marcos Santilli/Earthscan.

Printed and bound in Great Britain by
Cox & Wyman Ltd., Reading

British Library Cataloguing in Publication Data

The Vanishing forest : the human consequences of deforestation : a
    report for the Independent Commission on International
    Humanitarian Issues.
    1. Clear-cutting
    I. Independent Commission on International Humanitarian
    Issues   II. La Déforestation. *English*
    333.75   SD418

    ISBN 0-86232-631-1
    ISBN 0-86232-632-X Pbk

Contents

The Independent Commission on International Humanitarian Issues

Co-Chairmen:
Sadruddin Aga Khan (Iran)   Hassan bin Talal (Jordan)

Members:

Susanna Agnelli	(Italy)
Talal Bin Abdul Aziz Al Saud	(Saudi Arabia)
Paulo Evaristo Arns, Vice-Chairman	(Brazil)
Mohammed Bedjaoui	(Algeria)
Henrik Beer, Treasurer	(Sweden)
Luis Echeverria Alvarez	(Mexico)
Pierre Graber	(Switzerland)
Ivan Head	(Canada)
M. Hidayatullah	(India)
Aziza Hussein	(Egypt)
Manfred Lachs	(Poland)
Robert McNamara	(USA)
Lazar Mojsov	(Yugoslavia)
Mohamed Mzali, Vice-Chairman	(Tunisia)
Sadako Ogata, Vice-Chairman	(Japan)
David Owen	(United Kingdom)
Willibald P. Pahr, Vice-Chairman	(Austria)
Shridath S. Ramphal	(Guyana)
Ru Xin	(China)
Salim A. Salim	(Tanzania)
Léopold Sédar Senghor	(Senegal)
Soedjatmoko	(Indonesia)
Desmond Tutu	(South Africa)
Simone Veil	(France)
Gough Whitlam	(Australia)

Secretary General, ex-officio member:
Zia Rizvi (Pakistan)

Other ICIHI Reports

FAMINE: A Man-Made Disaster? (Pan Books, London/Sydney, 1985). Other language editions: Arabic, French, Italian, Japanese, Portuguese, Serbo-Croatian and Spanish.

THE ENCROACHING DESERT (Zed Books, London, 1986). Other language editions: Arabic and French.

STREET CHILDREN; A Growing Urban Tragedy (Weidenfeld & Nicolson, London, 1986). Other language editions: Arabic, French, Japanese and Spanish.

Other reports to be published in 1986 include:
  Humanitarian Norms and Armed Conflicts
  Refugees
  Disappeared Persons
  Statelessness
  Autochthonous People

Foreword

Over the millennia spanned by the history of mankind, agriculture has been developed to the detriment of forests. Forests have been destroyed by fire or axe and their resources squandered. Shadowy underbrush, suspected of harbouring a myriad dangers, has been replaced by the countryside and savanna. The apparent disorder of forests has been replaced by monotonous pastures and the established system of cultivation. Deforestation has thus long been considered a major manifestation of civilization.

Urban dwellers of the provinces of Ancient Rome were not the only ones to attribute to an area and its population a value inversely proportional to its distance from a city. Gardens, fields, pastures and forests were valued in decreasing order. Throughout the history of civilization, man has superimposed his own hierarchy of values on the physical layout of the land. Inhabitants of forests and their vicinities have always been relegated to the bottom rungs of these socio-centric ladders. They are sometimes so neglected as to be forgotten altogether. Many recent deforestation studies have failed even to mention those whose livelihoods depend upon the forest, and whose death results from its destruction. It is as if nature were to be preserved for its own sake and not managed in relation to mankind's present and future needs. From such a narrow point of view, neither the forest nor the societies it shelters is distinguished from trees.

Forests have long and abundantly supplied rural and

urban areas with construction materials and wood for fuel, with game, fruit, forage, bark for tanning hides and dyeing fabrics, and ingredients for medicinal preparations. As these resources ceased to appear limitless in temperate countries as a result of population growth and the reduction of forest expanse through deforestation, new rules of conduct became necessary. Hence the emergence of legal restrictions on the use of forests and their resources, building regulations to economize wood, 'economical furnaces' in 18th century Europe, new industrial energy sources (coal, steam, electricity), changes in crop rotations and the gradual disappearance of fallow land.

New forest regulations were the focus of bitter social strife in Europe. The reduction of forest rights in southern and western Germany was one of the causes of the peasant revolt which bathed the dawn of Lutherism in blood.

Large-scale use of forest resources is a recent development in tropical countries. Its consequences there are more severe than in temperate countries owing to the far greater number of people living in and off the forest. These people, existing on the fringes of the cultural, economic and political structures of society, have little power to make their voices heard and defend their rights. Traditional forest dwellers in tropical and equatorial areas are vulnerable to illnesses introduced by immigrants while, inversely, the newcomers succumb to diseases native to tropical forests. Neither group has the time to develop sufficient immunity. Moreover, the soil loses its natural fertility as a result of deforestation far more rapidly under tropical climatic conditions than in temperate zones.

This explains why the deterioration of tropical forests is in many respects irreversible. The soil becomes sterile or is carried away by erosion. Animal and plant species are lost forever. Forest deterioration and its side effects bring conflict in their wake. Concepts, priorities and plans collide as different communities enter into contact with one another. The very speed with which changes occur causes considerable human suffering.

Each tropical country has its specific ecological, social and economic problems. Detailed national economic development plans specify the number of square metres to be felled, the areas to be created for plantations and the funds required for the purpose. Planners often view forests as mere wood-supplying machines. Of course, cellulose can be produced through intensive cultivation of rapid-growing species on plantations set up near industrial centres where the demand is greatest. A genuine forestry policy – rare in tropical countries today – must never lose sight of the survival needs of tropical forest dwellers.

The use of tropical forest resources is one of the major socio-economic developments of this century. The example set by a country like Malaysia despite the numerous obstacles faced shows that a rational use of forests stands to serve the interests of the majority of the population. Other countries, on the contrary, have seriously undermined their forest resources by banking heavily on industrialization and international trade. Certain tropical countries, owing to a very rapidly deteriorating environment, have exhausted their forest resources altogether. In such cases, forestry policy must focus on halting the deterioration and, insofar as possible, reversing the trend with the participation of the populations concerned. In any event, the vital interests of these populations must lie at the heart of any forestry policy. Moreover, it must never be forgotten that the decisions made today carry consequences for generations to come. Trees, like societies, need time to develop.

The clearing and transformation of forests often constitute an integral part of development. All too often, however, a disproportionate amount of deforestation costs are borne by the most deprived segments of the population, namely the indigenous peoples and the poor settlers driven to the forests by rural poverty.

Tropical forests and their inhabitants thus pay the price for agricultural policies designed to satisfy the needs of a minority rather than to ensure employment and a steady food supply for all. A study of the humanitarian aspects of deforestation not only points to the weaknesses and errors inherent in agricultural policies, but also calls into question energy policies. Well-known methods exist for economizing wood, improved and inexpensive furnaces have been developed and alternative sources of low-cost energy are available.

Underscoring this lack of political will should be no excuse to avoid broaching its underlying reasons. In our opinion, it is the failure to attribute a major role to humanitarian considerations at the national and international levels in both the short and long term which explains why necessary policies have not been elaborated or implemented.

This is why the Independent Commission on International Humanitarian Issues has undertaken the task of sensitizing public opinion as well as political leaders to the suffering of those who, without power and without a voice, pay the price of mis-development. This report is a modest step in that direction. It is hoped that it will inspire more appropriate projects and pave the way for the implementation of wiser and more humane policies before it is too late for forests and forest dwellers.

Sadruddin Aga Khan
Co-Chairman of ICIHI

Editorial Note

Many scientific studies of tropical deforestation have appeared over the past few years. The Independent Commission felt, however, that the humanitarian aspects of the increasing disappearance of tropical forests, and in particular the welfare and health of populations directly concerned, have not been adequately addressed. We requested Professor D. Poore of the University of Oxford to look specifically into these aspects. He was assisted in his work by D. Burns and R. Van der Giessen. The Commission also benefited from reports prepared by the International Union for the Conservation of Nature (IUCN) with its support.

The comments made by the members of the Commission, in particular those participating in its Working Group on Disasters, are reflected in the Report. It was reviewed by P. Bifani, P. Spitz and other members of the Secretariat of the Commission. B. Palmer, M. El Kouhene and D. Topali helped in its technical preparation.

We wish to thank R. Molteno and Zed Books for their valuable assistance in the publication of the Report.

Any income from sales of this book will be devoted entirely to research on related humanitarian issues.

H. Beer
Convenor, ICIHI Working Group
on Disasters.

Z. Rizvi
Secretary-General

Geneva, April 1986

13

Introduction

The Humanitarian Aspects of Tropical Deforestation

The theme of this report is the effect of tropical deforestation on man: on individual men and women, some of them amongst the poorest of the earth, living on tropical forest lands. Their numbers are growing, and their forest resource is shrinking. These changes are happening at an increasingly rapid pace. Governments and business alike continue to plan and invest, but their calculations do not seem to allow for the fundamental economic and ecological constraints on the natural resource system. Ecologists attempt to protect the most valuable ecological sites, but their efforts seem futile before the force of economic needs and the expansion of human societies. Caught between the real constraints of the natural world and the rapid expansion of human needs for land and forest products, individual men and women are suffering the many and cruel effects of the degradation of tropical forest lands, a humanitarian problem that our policies have failed to control.

The Dwindling Forest

About 30 million km^2 of the land-surface of the tropics may be classed as forest land: about two-thirds of the total land-surface of the countries concerned. This natural resource is one of the great capital assets available to man. For many of the people living in and around the forest, it is virtually the only capital they have. The fate of these forest lands, and of the people who live upon them, is a subject of great and increasing humanitarian concern.

Of these 30 million km^2, about 12 million are still covered in closed forest, much of which benefits from a tropical moist climate. This is the tropical moist forest, an area boasting an extraordinary wealth of plant, animal and insect species, many of them still unknown and unstudied by man. Few people live in the natural closed forest, but many parts of it have been cleared and settled, and much of what remains is being severely disrupted by human activities.

Fourteen million km^2 are open forest and shrubland: *cerrado*, wooded savanna, areas of grassland where many communities live, hunt, or graze their herds. Four million km^2 are forest fallows, areas recently farmed which have been abandoned or left to regenerate naturally. In and around all these areas are the farms of today, some of them permanent farms on fertile soils, others destined to be abandoned in their turn as their occupants move on in search of better land.

It has been estimated that 0.6% of forest lands are being deforested every year: a phenomenon which is worrying in itself, since by the year 2000 a further 10% of forest capital will have been eaten away. But this outright deforestation is merely one aspect of a far greater problem, the *degradation* of tropical forest lands. As forest areas are logged, burnt, grazed, farmed and fallowed they may still be classed as forest; but in many cases their resilience is steadily being decreased, their soils eroded and impoverished, the diversity of their natural life curtailed. In large areas, the climate itself may be changing.

A Growing Population

It has been estimated that 140 million people now live in and around the closed forest. Just 1-2% of these are tribal, hunter-gatherer groups: descendants of larger communities who have lived in harmony with the forest for many centuries, but whose numbers have declined dramatically with the expansion of modern agricultural and industrial societies. Many of the rest are indigenous forest farmers. Often with a long tradition of successful shifting cultivation behind them, and capable of farming the forest sustainably, they are now increasingly forced to change their practices and to shorten their fallow rotations because of population pressures and economic demands. Finally, there are the new colonists — landless peasants, ranchers, logging and construction workers and large transnational corporations who have had little time to adapt to the tropical forest environment.

The population of tropical forest countries is projected to rise by 60-65% by the year 2000, but the number of these forest inhabitants may double or treble by that time, as ever increasing numbers of landless peasants move in from other areas. Yet the present area of tropical forest is scarcely enough to provide cultivable land for the existing population if shifting cultivation methods are used. These people must find ways to husband their individual plots of land sustainably — not to farm it for two or three years and then move on — or there will simply not be enough land to go round.

Forests have been the green frontier of mankind since time immemorial — a seemingly limitless resource for human expansion. With their supply of timber, fuelwood, game, and a rich variety of other products they were, and are, a crucial source of raw materials for human society. But increasingly we are realizing that they offer more than that. They offer more land when we need it; they balance and manage our water supplies and the flow of our rivers; they are a major force in determining our climate.

Many ancient civilizations would not have developed without the availability of forests and their products, and many of them decayed or even disappeared after depletion of these forests.

Now, on a much wider scale, we are faced with the prospect that the 'permanent renewable resource' can be exhausted. The forest degradation may in many ways be irreversible: soil is lost to erosion; animal and plant species disappear forever.

As degradation and its effects come rapidly into focus, conflicts emerge. Conflicts of ideas, priorities and plans; tensions on the ground, as different communities meet and their interests conflict; and suffering of many sorts, associated with the speed with which change is taking place.

A Conflict of Ideas, A Conflict of People

(1) Four questions are now being asked about this rate of forest destruction. First, there are those who question the economic wisdom of the way in which forest lands are being transformed for economic ends. Are we eating the seed corn; are we destroying the natural resource that should be tomorrow's economic base?

(2) Then there are those who question the irreversible interference with nature. Are we losing genetic resources at an unacceptable rate? Are we jeopardizing our planet's climate and its life-support systems? Are we deliberately creating an increasing danger of disastrous floods?

(3) What will become of the indigenous people of the forest? What is their fate as their habitat is destroyed and their way of life changed by the colonizers of the forest?

(4) What should be the role of the transnational corporations in forest development?

The debate on the future of the world's tropical forests has tended to be conceptual, conducted through learned papers and in conference halls. On the ground, the debate is carried out in a different way: it is lived out, in the suffering of individuals and in tensions between communities.

A Fight for Land: Different groups are carrying out pre-emptive transformations of the forest lands, without waiting for a consensus. Loggers over-exploit concessions: it is too late to save the trees. Dams inundate huge river-basins: communities must move. Landless peasants colonize the side of a new forest highway: too late for a settlement plan. Ranchers set fire to forest farms, transnational corporations move into the forest to raise cattle and open up the area to new landless peasants. Large or small, these acts are a battle for control of land. In the process of change, this competition for common property involves constant displacement and disruption, above all for the poor. As the limits of land availability approach, the pressure of conflict increases.

Conflict of Cultures: As communities migrate and expand, they come into contact with one another. Their traditions may have been valid before, defining the limits of a sustainable society. When groups with different traditions meet, these traditions conflict, and the ways of past generations have to be called in question. One group has 'sacred groves'; another group does not respect them. A logging team has no resistance to forest diseases; a tribal group has no resistance to the common cold. Techniques are brought in from other societies: bulldozers which compact and erode the soil; cattle with no resistance to sleeping-sickness. Within his own culture, each individual's actions may seem natural and justified, but in conditions of migration and contact the rules must be redefined.

Major Environmental Effects: Environmental damage is now resulting in disasters of unprecedented scale. Deforestation of the Andes catchment area by poor highland peasants and forest farmers turned the rains into a wave of floods and landslides of exceptional severity. The same year, in Indonesia, fires burnt a vast area of forest rendered vulnerable by selective logging and agricultural clearance.

Poverty and Malnutrition: Crops cultivated on the lateritic soils of much of the tropics are mostly deficient in protein: natural forest products such as bush-meat can make good that deficiency, for as long as the forest is there. When land is cleared, burning off the vegetation gives a short-term boost to fertility, but after a few years even the calorie-producing potential is lost as the soil is leached by rains. Fifty head of cattle on a 50-hectare holding in Latin America can provoke leaching and erosion just as fast. Debilitating disease and declining yields from the soil combine to sap labour productivity. Markets for produce are in many cases distant: intermediaries take the lion's share of the market price. Smallholders sink into a vicious circle of poverty and declining yields. Women and children bear an increasing proportion of the workload, collecting food and fuel and selling their labour.

In Chapter 1 we look at some of the main ways in which deforestation is connected with hardship and suffering for people in tropical forest lands. Chapter 2 discusses the different kinds of forest and their potential value. Chapter 3 highlights some ways in which *economic development can and must be supplemented by vigorous action to improve the welfare of forest people and to protect the forest resources* which they need to build their livelihood. Chapter 4 examines in particular the health problems of indigenous or migrant populations living in the forest environment or in recently deforested areas.

1. Humanitarian Aspects of Tropical Deforestation

Up until now tropical deforestation has been seen as a matter of ecological and economic concern. In this chapter, we set these issues on one side and look at seven aspects in which tropical deforestation is clearly a matter of humanitarian concern: ways in which deforestation can be seriously damaging to the health, welfare and future prospects of people living on tropical forest lands.

The nature of the forest resource and the kinds of problem which occur vary a great deal from one area to another: in later chapters we identify the types of situation which are most critical for people's welfare.

The impacts of deforestation on human life and well-being are many, and often extremely indirect: some may as yet be unknown to any of us. We have chosen these seven aspects to illustrate how the sum of human activities in forest areas can be directly harmful to the common interest.

Health: The Front Line

Deforestation in tropical forest areas raises serious health problems which can only be resolved by sound forest management, settlement planning, adequate infrastructure and health care.

To a certain extent, traditional forest dwellers have adapted to their environment and become immune to potential forest diseases.

But forest conversion attracts new settlers who are not immune to typical forest patogens such as yellow fever, filariasis, African and American trypanosomiasis, leishmaniasis and scrub typhus.

Conversely, immigrants bring into the tropical forest ecosystem other diseases against which forest dwellers have no immunity.

Deforestation also brings about a change in vector habitat and in the relationship between the vector and its environment, which in turn modifies risk patterns. Clearing may destroy some breeding sites and therefore have a positive effect, but it can also induce less desirable changes in vector behaviour. For instance, mosquitoes or sand-flies which used to feed on primates, rodents and other forest animals find fewer potential animal hosts and have a greater tendency to feed on human beings. There are also cases where forest clearing eliminates the vector's natural enemies or replaces non-vector by vector species.

Finally, the concentration of settlers without adequate sanitation creates additional health problems, mainly the proliferation of intestinal parasites.

Chapter 4 on Health and Deforestation provides an overview of a number of different diseases associated with tropical forests and with the clearance of those forests.

In this chapter we take malaria as an example. This is possibly the most serious disease and major cause of morbidity and child mortality in the tropics and is present in virtually all areas currently being deforested. Globally there are some 5 million new cases per year: 1 million African children are dying of it annually. A total of 1.2 *billion* people live in risk areas. Yet what is not widely known is that malaria is largely a man-made disease. Agricultural colonists are one of the major carriers of malaria and in their drive to clear and settle new areas of forest they create new endemic foci and rapidly extend the limits of the disease to people and places it had not reached before.

Eradication of Disease and Population Growth
Tropical peoples have on the whole developed a considerable resistance to malaria. Those who survive an infection are nevertheless subject to periodic attacks which are now

widely recognized as a major depressing influence – along with protein deficiency, heat and other factors – on labour productivity. As a result, the latent economic potential of malaria eradication is enormous. At the time of the first malaria eradication programmes in the tropics, the fear was expressed that successful eradication, despite its beneficial effect on productivity and its potential for saving human lives, would open the path to explosive population growth, which was seen as a potential economic cost. The point is that in the short term, disease eradication tends to increase population growth, and thus make it all the more important that the carrying capacity of the natural environment be nurtured and respected.

Few people would deny that improved health care in general has indeed contributed to the rapid population growth of the post-war period. But it is also now clear that a direct relation between improved health care and population growth does not exist. Malaria was largely eradicated by spraying in Sri Lanka in 1947 (although there has been a more recent resurgence).[1] Since then, Sri Lanka has seen a quite remarkable fall in fertility: it now has the lowest total fertility rate of any low-income country except China.[2] Sri Lanka – at $300 per capita annual income still a very poor country – stands out as an example of the fact that *social* development can be more important than mere economic growth in influencing population growth.[3]

Malaria and Forest Management
In all countries, malaria can only be eradicated by adopting diversified control measures of primary health care which must be an integral part of development programmes. Vector control aims at reducing contact between vectors and human populations, primarily by reducing vector populations, which in turn can be achieved by reducing or disturbing vector habitats. A number of the many different species of the *anopheles* mosquito which transmit malaria thrive in a disturbed forest environment, e.g. *anopheles balbacensis*. This species is growing rapidly in importance, and spreading northwards from South East Asia into wide areas of Asia where malaria had been very successfully controlled.

Unfortunately more and more people are living in or around partially disrupted forests where this malaria vector thrives. One of the most effective ways of managing this vector is to clear-fell the forest along suspected streams, strand pools and tractor ruts in the hinterland of villages. But this conflicts seriously with sound forest management and can, especially on riverbanks, accelerate erosion. It has been suggested that one should locate villages at least one kilometer away from the forest because of the limited flight range of the mosquito.[4]

Health Care for Forest Settlers

Colonization of forest areas tends to occur in remote areas isolated from public health systems and without benefit of environmental vector management. In particular, official resettlement programmes are generally conducted in a spirit of urgency and 'on the cheap'; they do not always include safe water supplies nor the necessary measures to avoid unhealthy conditions such as stagnating water, garbage and bad housing and sanitary facilities. In general, low standards of living provide circumstances in which many diseases and their vectors can thrive.[5]

While the vectors develop resistance to insecticides, the parasites develop resistance to drugs — mainly chloroquine — generally used for therapy and prophylaxis. This increases the technical and administrative difficulties faced in eradication campaigns mainly because of inadequate infrastructure.

In many resettlement and colonization projects, expenditure on health is not high enough to ensure that adequate care will be taken of the health of colonists living in deforested or degraded areas of the tropical forest zone. The commitment to an objective of adequate health care is political. National governments must accept responsibility for the health of their remotest citizens.

Deforestation and the Welfare of Mothers and Children

Mothers and small children are often the first to suffer in conditions of forest poverty. Not only are small children in no position to defend their own interests, but their mothers' childbearing and childraising role makes them more dependent — dependent on men, dependent on the immediate social and family group, and dependent on the readiness of the wider society to recognize their special needs.

A woman who bears six children is either pregnant or responsible for children under the age of four for an average of well over 10 years of her life. At a rough calculation, around a third of all women of childbearing age in the tropics are having to cope with this constraint at any one time.[6] In many situations of economic hardship, natural disasters and periods of seasonal stress, the social group will be equipped and willing to shelter mothers and young children from the worst. But the social disruption which is a feature of much tropical deforestation often exposes them to degrees of hardship and humiliation quite unthinkable in more stable peasant communities.

Short-term out-of-village labour is frequent in areas of deforestation: in logging, mining and infrastructure projects, in seasonal activities on plantations, and in the generalized, urgent search for sources of cash income. A household relying on this type of work must choose between breaking up the family unit for substantial periods of time or subjecting mother and children to socially unstable, dangerous and unhealthy living conditions in temporary settlements.

Long-distance migration of entire household units inevitably deprives women and children of the support provided by a stable village bound together by ties of kinship.

Lack of a modern social infrastructure in terms of education provision, contraceptive availability, and health care is typical of many areas of planned and unplanned colonization. Some countries such as Ecuador have developed remarkable systems for ensuring the provision of health care even to the remotest areas. But extension of health care to isolated communities lowers the size of population that a health care unit can serve, and therefore leads to a substantial increase in unit costs of health care. Only the strongest of humanitarian ethics can ensure that urban centres of administrative power respect the basic needs of the human communities that are the most remote and thus the hardest to serve.[7]

Deforestation is often also accompanied by a sharp rise in the burden of economic activities placed on mothers and small children. The fuelwood crisis is widely associated in the public mind with images of mothers and children walking long distances to cut and carry heavy loads of fuel. Deforestation also tends to increase time required to collect non-wood forest products traditionally collected by women. As a general rule, collection times are longer in open than in closed forest, even where the forest has been severely degraded: in the Nigerian moist forest belt, fuelwood collection may typically take one hour per week, whereas in the savanna belt it may take one hour per day.[8] Fuelwood shortage varies enormously from one locality to another, both in and outside the tropical forest zone, and generalizations are difficult. For Nepal, for example, estimates of household fuelwood collection times vary from 4 hours per week to 22 hours per week from one village to another.[9]

Deforestation, and fuelwood shortage in particular, can greatly increase the economic strain on poor households. It is a depressing feature of human society that so much of this strain is borne by those least equipped to bear it. There is little that benevolent intervention can do in the short term to improve the lot of mothers and small children in communities − whether in big cities or on remote frontiers − where their needs are not adequately respected by a male-dominated society. Many of the tribal groups whose last forest strongholds are now being invaded have much more humane attitudes to maternity than those of the dominant culture.[10]

On the other hand, the way in which women have led the campaign of the Chipko movement to prevent the felling of trees in the Himalayas is only one example of the increasing willingness of women to defend their environment, if necessary against the opposition of their own sons and husbands.[11]

Humane action to protect women's rights and to respect their particular needs is very hard to pursue: the fragmented imposition of a 'modern' social code or a 'modern' social infrastructure may often be counter-productive. Certainly, no amount of forest conservation can remedy the hardship which social norms impose. But sound, caring management of the natural environment, by giving migrants economic security and the time and stability to develop stable communities, can make a powerful contribution to the welfare of women and children.

Malnutrition: A Growing Problem

Sub-Saharan Africa's per capita food production declined by 10% between 1970 and 1979. Thanks to rising imports and food aid, the average calorie intake was held stable at about 94% of recognized minimum requirements (EEC, 1982). The shortfall was felt hardest in the Sahel (85% of requirement). But Central Africa, an area much of which is covered in moist forest, achieved an average calorie intake of only 92% of requirements.[12] These people are not suffering from famines: their climate is humid and reliable for much of the year. Their problem is one of persistent inadequacy of food supplies and chronic malnutrition.

In much of the tropical forest zone, and in particular in Latin America, food deficiency is related to a flagrantly unequal distribution of wealth and income. This is frequently compounded by an agricultural emphasis on export products. Cattle-ranching, in particular, is not only inefficient and inappropriate as a source of calories but is also associated with severe inequality of income at the national and international level. In many tropical countries, nevertheless, average per capita food availability has been stable or increasing, and the natural environment has not been seen as a major obstacle to basic nutritional goals. Yet the link between deforestation and declining food production is very strong. Nepal, which has lost one-third of its legally reserved forests since 1947 and now has only 12% of its land surface under tree cover, has seen its per capita food production fall by 17% since 1970. Haiti, only 2% of whose forests remain, has suffered a 15% fall in per capita food production in the same period.

In the last five to ten years, a new and extremely worrying trend has emerged. A number of tropical countries apparently well-endowed with resources and with a predominantly agricultural economy[13] have been registering sharp falls in per capita food production. Zaire has registered a fall of 13% during the 1970s. In Central Africa, the decline in food production cannot be ignored as a major humanitarian concern.

Forest clearance in these countries does not and will not ensure increased agricultural production. Rather, it is an environmentally damaging symptom of an inefficient agricultural system.

The humanitarian problem that this poses is widely misunderstood. Humanitarian assistance to peoples suffering from hunger in arid parts of the world is justified by the obvious physical evidence of desertification. Yet the lateritic soils characteristic of much of the moist tropics are an important but less obvious handicap. Foods produced on lateritic soils tend to be relatively rich in carbohydrates but poor in protein. Protein deficiency may constitute a serious nutritional problem even when minimum calorie requirements are met.[14] In addition, attempts to intensify and extend agricultural production by clearing moist forest areas have led to compaction and further leaching of soils until even carbohydrate production declines. It has been shown that tropical forest dwellers suffer from protein-energy malnutrition and severe anaemia as a result of protein, vitamin A, iodine and iron deficiencies.

Because climate and agricultural production in the moist tropics are relatively stable, the acute famines characteristic of the arid and semi-arid zones do not occur. In contrast, unspectacular malnutrition in the moist forest zone, enhanced by debilitating diseases, saps the will to self-help and yet fails to arouse the concern of the international community.

Tribal Peoples: The Myth of the Vast Emptiness

The 'myth of the vast Amazonian emptiness' described by Chase-Smith (1982) is a common feature of forest development plans in all parts of the tropics. For example, the Peruvian Pichis-Palcazu project was designed to resettle poor families from Lima in Peruvian Amazonia, but they may soon realize that the forest was not as empty as it seemed. Low population density in tropical forest areas is often not so much a sign of emptiness but more a sign that indigenous peoples are living in balance with their environment. This low population density, however, provides an excuse for the predatory expansion of an urban and peri-urban system incapable of ministering to its own needs or of absorbing its own growth.

At a conservative estimate, 140 million people in the world live in or on the edges of closed tropical forest (Myers 1980). A separate estimate puts the number of tribal people living in relative isolation throughout the world at 200 million (Goodland, 1982) of which many are forest-dwellers. Although the available statistics are very approximate, it is clear that tribal farmers and hunter-gatherers constitute a significant minority of those directly affected by forest development and deforestation.

The degree of cultural resilience of the different groups, and the extent to which their mode of life has been disrupted, is highly variable. For as long as there is an indigenous culture, attacks on that culture are a matter of humanitarian concern. But the problem does not disappear if and when the group is irrevocably disrupted or acculturated. The humanitarian problem becomes a more individual one as members of the group show themselves more or less capable of adaptation. Chronic alcoholism amongst North American Indians is one powerful illustration of the long-term effects of partial acculturation. In some developing countries this acculturation is easier when the dominant culture has in fact partly grown out of the indigenous culture, as in Malaysia or Ecuador. However, in countries such as Brazil and Zaire, long after the old way of life has disappeared almost without trace, members of tribal minorities may still suffer from a vicious inequality of opportunity.

Some forest-dwellers, such as the Kuna Indians of the Caribbean coast of Panama, have shown a remarkable capacity to adapt to modern society, while conserving in the meantime their tribal traditions and culture. But most forest tribal groups, after suffering a generalized assault on their land rights and, in many cases, on their basic human rights as well, will not be capable of such adaptation.

The probability that clearance of any tropical forest area will affect an indigenous tribal group is *remarkably high*. The land of every tribal group in the world has been placed under the overall ownership of nation states, often arbitrarily, and frequently before these powers have had any effective control over remote areas. Tribal land rights subsequently written into national legislation are rarely defined after due consultation with the groups concerned.[15] The economic activities of indigenous groups do not necessarily lead them to occupy physically all the land which is traditionally theirs. 30,000 Kuna, for example, lay claim to a 200-kilometre band of the Caribbean watershed of Panama. Although this area is smaller than that occupied by the Kuna in the past, it is an ecologically discrete area: any incursion into it is liable to affect their ecological, as well as their cultural, security even if no Kuna member is physically displaced. In fact, the Kuna have their main settlements around estuaries or on islands along the coast. In order to protect their territory, the Kuna have made a conscious decision to establish a permanent settlement on the inland edge of their territory. Their territorial rights are recognized by the central government, which has declared a nature reserve at the critical point of entrance to Kuna lands at Udirbi. In order to protect these rights, teams of Kuna now patrol the edge of the forest several times a week at Udirbi to prevent the influx of poor colonists.[16] Recognition and respect of tribal land-rights in such cases is an urgent and difficult humanitarian problem.

It is indeed a common phenomenon that forest groups live on the edges of their traditional homeland rather than under the forest canopy. The Miskito population of the Caribbean coast of Nicaragua live mainly in pine savanna on the edge of their forest territory. The Nambiquara of Southern Rondônia in Brazil traditionally have their settlements in savanna with only their gardens within the forest of the valley below. Encroachment frequently damages first the interface between two ecological zones, which is in many cases the most valuable ecological niche for indigenous groups.

Territorial encroachment is not necessarily accompanied by physical conflict. South of the Nyong river in Southern Cameroon, communities of the dominant Bantu ethnic group are now settled on sites still showing signs of occupation by the Pygmy minority, which has steadily retreated in the face of the shifting agricultural expansion. But when an indigenous group is unwilling to retreat or has nowhere to retreat to, it is also frequently prey to human rights abuse. The Inter-American Commission on Human Rights reports many cases of violence to Indians living in South and Central American forests,[17] and one authority maintains that all cases reported of human rights abuse involving tropical forest dwellers are connected with frontiers of colonization.

Migration and Displacement: 'We Can't Eat Houses'

Migration within a given territory, both of pastoralists and of shifting agricultural cultivators, is a common feature in traditional societies. However, migration away from traditional areas and over long distances is also currently a widespread phenomenon in tropical forest areas. As we discuss below, this may take the form of planned and implemented resettlement programmes, of spontaneous migration before and after official resettlement, or of spontaneous migration to the sites of other development projects. It may often be entirely unconnected with official development planning. Although involuntary migration may present the most severe problems, households which take the risk of migrating voluntarily are not necessarily better equipped to cope with their new environment. In displacement of any kind, adaptation to a new natural environment and negotiation with new neighbours go hand in hand.

For many years the Indonesian Government has been resettling Javanese families on the sparsely inhabited Outer Islands. Since 1969 the Transmigration Programme has resettled about half a million families on land formerly occupied by moist, and largely virgin, tropical forest. Around 130,000 of these households are already known to be living in conditions of dire poverty as a result of the exhaustion of soil fertility caused by soil compaction, erosion and lowering of available soil nutrient content. This has happened within a period of three to five years after land clearance. Some areas settled in this way have subsequently been vacated altogether.

In 1980, the Peruvian Government announced the Pichis-Palcazu Special Project, involving resettlement of 150,000 people from Lima in an area of the Upper Amazon basin already occupied by Amuesha and Campa tribal groups and a similar number of settlers. The project has been the subject of much discussion and has not been fully implemented. The preparatory works carried out have facilitated access for individual settlers whose numbers are already straining the area's fragile ecology and primitive infrastructure without there being a full development project in support.

In addition, the feasibility stage of any project within tropical forests (whether it be a highway, mining, or hydro-electric project) is itself likely to encourage inward migration. The project for a major dam in 'Silent Valley' in Kerala State, India's best-preserved area of moist forest, was finally aborted because of public conservationist pressure: but not before a hopeful colony had formed on the site of the proposed works. Similar settlements occurred with highway development projects in Amazonia.

It matters little in practice whether resettlement is planned or not. The more ambitious 'planned' schemes such as the Polonoroeste project in Rondônia in Brazil cannot fulfil expectations since the logistical problems of fair and rational land allocation and the creation of social infrastructure are too formidable. Resettlement plans such as those in Ecuador and Peru which rely heavily on cheap credit incentives frequently cause more problems than they solve: the credit is used to purchase cattle which rapidly exhaust soil fertility and lead to severe erosion. Resettlement schemes on a more modest scale, such as those used to reduce population pressure on the Western Highlands of Cameroon, cannot command the attention of central government and sink into poverty, unsung even by journalists, in forgotten corners of the savanna.

When people migrate spontaneously they may fare no better. As their farms fail they are obliged to move on, ceaselessly shifting the limits of cultivation. But this should not be called 'shifting cultivation'. True shifting cultivation is a viable form of land-use based on a traditional knowledge of the ecological constraints of the area. Migration is frequently mere displacement, and presents a baffling problem for the migrant. For example:

> An Indian who wants to make a bow or kill a wild boar does not wander randomly through the forest, but goes directly to the trees which furnish wood for bows or the salt licks frequented by wild boars. A profound knowledge of the area is essential for survival. Thus, if a group is moved away from its traditional area, its chances for survival are jeopardized. Even if the new area is ecologically similar to the group's homeland, its members may starve before they can find necessary resources (Price, in *Cultural Survival* p. 62).

If the adaptation is so difficult for a traditional forest-dweller displaced to an ecologically similar area, it must come as no surprise that the migrant from afar has such difficulty in developing sustainable forms of land use.[18]

Some of the more successful resettlement schemes have involved intensive planning of cash-crop production such as rubber and copra. The Malaysian authorities have been able to offer a feasible economic base to resettled populations in remote parts of Peninsular Malaysia, Sarawak and Sabah. These remote settlements are, however, acutely dependent on the overstretched marketing system for signals as to the economic potential of their activity on the world market. Traditional settlements on the Peninsula are able to adjust the balance of cash-crop, kampong and market-garden activities from year to year. A remote settlement can only react to a slump in the rubber market by slaughter-tapping hevea trees to maintain income or by falling back on a subsistence mode for which it is ill-prepared.

The complex problems of the peasant colonist are less spectacular than those of the tribal groups which he threatens. It is easy to sympathize with the Kuna Indian in Panama patrolling the edges of his forest reserve. But the Panamanian colonist, caught in a pincer movement of the land-hungry cattle ranchers to the south and the reserve guards to the north, frequently finds himself in the most inhuman position of all.

That is why communities offered the possibility of relocation are frequently well-advised to sit it out, like the Guaymi, living on one of the world's largest proven copper reserves in the degraded and overpopulated moist forest zone of Western Panama (Gjording, 1981): 'They hear they are to be given new houses, but they don't know where and, they add, "We can't eat houses".'

Fragile Lands: One Man's Poverty, Another Man's Disaster

From November 1982 to June 1983 the entire coastal plain of north-west Latin America from Esmeraldas to Lima was subjected to floods. 671 deaths were directly attributed to the floods in Ecuador and Peru; an estimated 1.4 million people lost their homes or livelihoods. The floods caused material hardship to the majority of the coastal population and constituted a serious health hazard, particularly through contamination of water supplies.

The disaster was triggered by a recurring phenomenon, the *El Nino* current, which can be so strong that it disturbs the climatic balance along the Pacific coast of Latin America. In 1965 *El Nino* contributed, together with overfishing, to the decimation of the coastal anchovy fisheries. However, the torrential rains which it brought in 1983 fell on the Andean Pacific watershed which since 1965 has lost around 20% of its forests to outright deforestation, most of the remainder being severely degraded. Disastrous floods and landslides were the result.

Damage in the two countries from the 1983 floods was estimated at $1.2 billion; most of this was due to flood-induced landslides and flooding of river basins. The proportion of this damage directly related to deforestation and watershed degradation is difficult to estimate, but was undoubtedly a major element. Foreign contributions to disaster relief totalled $12.7 million in Ecuador and $84.7 million in Peru, where long-term development assistance programmes were disrupted and curtailed to mobilize funds for short-term relief.

Little development assistance, however, has been directed towards forest conservation, reforestation and watershed protection in Ecuador and Peru. In 1980, the US Agency for International Development committed $0.5 million to a forestry component of a $12 million rural development project in Ecuador, and $0.5 million to reforestation in Peru. In 1982 the World Bank committed another $0.5 million to a watershed protection component of a rural development project in Peru. These sums are pitiful in comparison with the total assistance flows to Ecuador and Peru over the period.

The problem of fragile lands is quite different from the problems of leaching and compaction of lowland tropical soils.[19] It is a global problem, transcending political frontiers and ecological zones. Floods affected 15.4 million people each year in the 1970s, an almost threefold increase over the 1960s. One of the worst hit areas is the Ganges-Brahmaputra plain, where in a few weeks in 1978 floods inundated 66,000 villages, drowned 2,000 people and killed 40,000 cattle and caused damage estimated at $2 billion. The area annually affected by floods averages 40 million hectares and this vulnerable area is still increasing. Every year more people come to live on the flood plains because they find fertile land there. The Indian Government estimated in 1978 that one in 20 people in India was vulnerable to flooding.

The flooding is clearly related to deforestation in the Himalayas. Prevention measures in India are projected to cost $100 million annually. Yet most of this will go to major engineering works such as dams and dykes in the lowlands. Only 1% will be spent on really preventive action: forest and watershed conservation and reforestation in the foothills and lower mountains of the Himalayas.

The fragile lands most vulnerable to deterioration are not, on the whole, made up of the lateritic soils which we connect with the forest zone malnutrition already discussed in this chapter. Mountain areas of the tropics tend either to have volcanic soils (e.g. in Western Cameroon, Rwanda and Burundi, parts of Indonesia and most of the Andes), or else to have much younger and more fertile soils which are not lateritic. The fragility of the land is much more strongly related to slope, the intensity of periodic rainfall and the agricultural and pastoral practices used. Poverty and insecurity of land rights exacerbate bad land use because costly soil conservation measures are not applied. This may result in a vicious circle of land degradation and increasing poverty: a process which is an everyday reality in the Andes, in the Himalayas and in the highlands of Central America.

Nepal has lost well over a third of its forests since the Private Forests (Nationalization) Act brought all forest under government control in 1957.[20] Real protection of the frail lands of the mountains must be part of an integral development of the area affected, and involve as a first step alleviation of the highlanders' poverty. Amongst their needs are forest plantations as a sure source of fuel; assistance in land conservation and pasture management; and above all, secure and equitable rights to the land.

Fire: The Undeclared Disaster

The economic and ecological effects of fire in tropical forest areas may not at first sight appear to be a subject for humanitarian concern. In the long term, they can be debilitating — and many countries are already experiencing this long term. In Haiti and the Dominican Republic, for example, fires have played a significant role in reducing an area of the tropical moist zone to a state of 'vegetation poverty', despite continuing high rainfall and once-fertile soil. In 1983, a forest fire in the Dominican Central Highlands inflicted severe damage to timber and soil over an area of 3,000 hectares, despite rapid and effective fire-fighting assistance from a foreign disaster relief agency. The people of this island can ill afford such damage, however localized.

Fires can affect very large areas. From mid-1983 to early 1984, forest fires raged in different parts of Indonesia. The most severely affected area was Eastern Kalimantan on the island of Borneo, where approximately 35,000 km^2 (an area larger than Belgium) was burnt in the region of Balikpapan. Most of this fire occurred in an area of tropical moist forest. It is widely considered that the fire would have been impossible in virgin forest conditions, even in an unusually dry year. The critical factor was in all probability the impact of human activity: in particular, selective logging and agricultural expansion over a number of years had opened wide gaps in the forest canopy and left inflammable detritus on the forest floor.

While tropical forest fires take few human lives and make few headlines, their indirect effects are hard to underestimate. Fire is an agent in almost all processes of deforestation and forest degradation, and deforestation on the contemporary scale would scarcely be possible without it. Controlled burning of vegetation offers a short-term increase in the availability of organic matter and nutrients for agriculture, and it is for this reason — as well as simply to clear land-surface — that fire is used throughout the world as an instrument of slash-and-burn agriculture. The increase in availability is won, however, at the expense of a deterioration in soil structure and a loss of some nutrients such as nitrogen which disperse into the atmosphere by combustion.

Much of the world's savanna has been created and is maintained by recurrent fires, as is the relative extent of tropical coniferous forest, as opposed to broad-leaved forest. Savannization is of particular importance since subsequent economic potential is heavily dependent on the type of savanna vegetation which results. Fire is mainly responsible for the maintenance and extension of unproductive imperata grass on abandoned agricultural land in tropical Asia. In tropical Africa, there are now more than two hectares of savanna for every hectare of closed forest, and sustainable use of this savanna is of critical importance where it borders on Sahelian zones. Proper fire control is essential for such sustainable use.

Recurrent dry-season fires — whether spontaneous or the result of slash-and-burn activity — can cause formidable damage to agricultural crops. This destruction is all the more important in the case of the woody plantation crops often found in the savanna zone and in areas of severely degraded forest. Coffee, cocoa and fruit tree plantations in the Ivory Coast, in an area once covered by moist forest, were badly damaged by fire in the 1983 dry season. The annual fire hazard has, along with a disturbed pattern of water collection, developed into a major depressing influence on the Ivorian economy.[21]

It is intentional that no attempt has been made here to distinguish between natural and man-made fires. Effective fire-control is extremely difficult in either case – for logistical reasons in the case of natural fire hazard, for sociological reasons in the case of man-made fires for clearance, hunting and other purposes. Whatever the causes, the combustion effect is the same, and wherever it occurs, an uncontrolled forest fire can develop into an undeclared disaster.

Notes

1. Only 17 cases of malaria were diagnosed in 1963 in Sri Lanka, but there was subsequently a resurgence, and 300,000 cases were diagnosed in 1974 (Klamarck 1976).

2. Population growth fell from 2.4% per annum in the 1960s to 1.7% in the 1970s. Births per woman by age 35 fell from 4.6 in the late 1950s to 2.9 in the early 1970s (Lightbourne et al. 1982).

3. Social development is, of course, hard to measure. At 85%, adult literacy is higher in Sri Lanka than in any low-income country except Vietnam (World Bank 1984).

4. 'The answer to malaria in most of the Tropics pending any new research successes appears to be combination programs including spraying, draining swamps, clearing of bush, and mass chemotherapy and chemoprophylaxis' (Klamarck 1976, p. 69). We are indebted to Dr Graham White for information on environmental management of malaria vectors.

5. The paradoxical fact that some diseases, such as malaria and leishmaniasis, are actually best remedied by clearing the forest and that other diseases, such as scrub typhus, only begin to thrive after clearing does not encourage sound development of forest land. Moreover, the highly ingenious mechanisms of disease transmission can cause unpleasant surprises during the implementation of a colonization project. Cases of an unknown or unexpected disease

may suddenly occur and pose a serious threat to a development project and those working on it.

6. Data from the World Fertility Survey show that an average of six children ever born is common for African women, although as many as 30% of these children will die before age 5 (the Lesotho case). In Asia and Latin America the average number of children ever born is somewhat lower (4.5 to 5 for countries studied). The estimates given in the text should be considered as orders of magnitude only.

7. It is paradoxically often the case that provision to remote areas leads to innovations in health care which may be both more effective and less costly than standard modern methods.

8. Ardayfio-Schandorf (1982), quoted in Cecelski (1984, unpublished). Cecelski provides a detailed assessment of the effects of fuelwood shortage on women's work patterns.

9. Leach, personal communication. One of the difficulties in survey data has been the wide variation in household size. The two Nepal estimates are from two different surveys amongst many, and the data are not necessarily compatible.

10. Cultural Survival (1984) provides a number of case-studies.

11. Cf. for example Agarwal and Anand, 1983.

12. Central Africa includes Burundi, Cameroon, Central African Republic, Congo, Gabon, Sao Tome and Principe, Rwanda and Zaire. It should be said that food production per capita and calorie intake statistics are not always reliable, though the general trends are unmistakable.

13. One of the more sophisticated analyses of carrying capacity was carried out as a part of the FAO project 'Land Resources for Populations of the Future'. The results suggest that no tropical forest country should exceed its theoretical carrying capacity before the end of the century. As Paul Harrison points out (Earthwatch 1983), FAO made the critical working assumption that all cultivable lands in each country would be devoted to basic food crops to maximize calorie intake. This raises important questions of environmental sustainability and social feasibility; more realistic — but still arbitrary — assumptions indicate that carrying capacity limits in some areas, even under best available technology, may be much closer to hand.

14. Klamarck (1976) has drawn attention to protein shortage. It is of course true that appropriate agricultural techniques can alleviate protein shortage even on poor lateritic soils, in particular through the use of tropical legumes, many of which are not indigenous species or traditionally accepted crops. It is ecologically often more appropriate to harness the protein resources of the natural environment which agriculture tends to destroy, such as bush-meat and other 'minor' forest products.

15. The Malay Reservations Enactment of 1913 provides an interesting case of consultation: 'Most of the reservations (in Perak) consisted of unoccupied land in the upland regions of the state where there were not only few conflicting interests to be considered but also the absence of a Malay population to take advantage of them. Apparently this incongruity did not cross the minds of government officials . . . What had begun as an attempt to preserve Malay land by restricting disposal rights had become, irrationally, an exercise in restricting cultivation rights, which in turn threatened the viability of the initial objective of the reserve policy' (Lim Teck Ghee 1977, pp. 113-116). Another problem was that much reserved land turned out to have been already irrevocably alienated. The Act of 1913 is thus one of the rare cases of tribal lands protection preceded by extensive consultation with tribal representatives. It raised the very difficult problem that the indigenous people may be enticed into disposing of traditional homelands for gain, and Malay leaders in fact strongly defended the right of their people to do so. The same problem resurfaced in the acrimonious Brazilian debate on the proposed emancipation of Indian communities in the 1970s (Cultural Survival 1979).

16. MacDonald, personal communication.

17. Cf. Inter-American Commission on Human Rights, 1982, p. 328: 'The Commission has studied with concern the repeated denunciations regarding aggression committed against Indians, who are usually victims of illegal means or trickery used in order to despoil them of their lands. Their physical destruction is even more serious, under the ceaseless thrust of entrepreneurs and explorers in the areas they inhabit. Acts of incredible abuse of force have been reported, in which entire settlements have been wiped out by aggressive invaders of the forests.'

18. By contrast, a 1976 survey of Indonesia's transmigration experience indicated that in this case spontaneous settlers had a higher standard of living than those who were part of the official programme. A number of explanations may be suggested, but one factor may well be the difference in land-clearing techniques used by spontaneous settlers and by the programme's contractors (Ross and Donovan 1984).

19. The concept of 'fragile lands' is beginning to receive more attention, particularly by USAID (1984), which puts a somewhat wider definition on the term. It would seem wise to separate the problems associated with laterization and those primarily attributable to slope, since the concomitant socio-economic and ecological factors are very different in the two cases.

20. Wallace (1982) points out that prior to the alienation of forest lands in 1957 many Nepalese communities operated viable forest protection systems on a decentralized basis. Undoubtedly population pressure and cumulative deterioration have also played a role.

21. Arnaud and Sournia (1980) give a detailed discussion. Existing Indonesian transmigration plans imply a rapid growth of settlements and population densities in Eastern Kalimantan in the coming years.

2. The Tropical Forest : A Resource for People

Tropical deforestation has been measured statistically: 0.64% per annum in tropical America, 0.61% in tropical Africa, 0.60% in tropical Asia, according to the most authoritative figures currently available.[1] This statistical uniformity belies the variety of conditions in which deforestation occurs, and threatens to dull our sense of the impact it can have on individual people's lives.

In this chapter we look at different reasons why people want to save forests, and the different types of forest they want to protect.

Types of Forest

29 million km^2 of the land surface of the tropics may be classed as forest land: about two-thirds of the total land surface of the countries concerned (FAO 1982). Of these 29 million km^2, about 11 million are still covered in *closed forest*, much of which benefits from a tropical moist climate. This is the tropical moist forest to which we return later in this chapter. Few people live under the closed forest, but many parts of it have been cleared and settled, and much of what remains has been more or less severely disrupted by human activities such as timber extraction.

Of the remaining 18 million km^2, 14 million are *open forest* and shrubland, including types of savanna, pasture and grassland which are partly wooded. The remaining 4 million km^2 are *forest fallow*, areas recently farmed which have been abandoned or left to regenerate naturally. In and around all these areas are the farms of today, some of them permanent farms on fertile soils, others destined to be abandoned in their turn as their occupants move on in search of better land.

Climate patterns may themselves be influenced by deforestation, as we discuss later. It is customary to class as tropical forest some areas outside the Tropics of Cancer and Capricorn, such as forested areas of Northern India and Nepal, which share some of the ecological and development problems characteristic of the tropical zone: we follow that convention in this report.

It is estimated that 0.6% of both closed and open forest are being deforested every year. Although this figure may seem low, it implies that a further 10% of the tropical forest will be deforested by the year 2000. But this outright deforestation is merely one aspect of a far greater problem, the *degradation* of tropical forest and tropical forest lands. As forest areas are logged, burnt, grazed, farmed and fallowed, their resilience is steadily being decreased, their soils eroded and impoverished, and the diversity of their natural life curtailed.

The humanitarian problems discussed in Chapter 1 affect different areas in very different ways. The forest's economic value as a timber reserve and as an ecological resource can be quite distinct from its real value to people and society as a whole. Perhaps 140 million people now live in and around the closed forest. Many more are affected by the way the forest is being converted; many live on lands which were once forested, and are no longer.

Tropical Deforestation: Reasons for Concern

Tropical forests are disappearing. Somewhere along the road to complete deforestation, people begin to place a high value on the remaining forest.

In most temperate countries, the area of forest cover has already declined to a point at which populations see clearly the value of the remaining forest, and are prepared to protect it. This time will come in the tropics, but if present trends are not reversed, it will inevitably come too late in many cases.[2] Such is the vulnerability of tropical soils to leaching, compaction and erosion under the play of tropical heat and rainfall, and such is the cumulative effect of population growth and economic change, that the forest destruction will be ecologically irreversible and, in many cases, complete.

Many people involved in different aspects of tropical conversion are now acutely worried about the consequences of deforestation.

Others see forests as a more or less inexhaustible source of raw materials, yet their importance goes far beyond the mere appropriation and use of timber, fruits, chemicals or animals.

The forest system fulfils extremely important protective, regulatory and productive functions both for the natural environment and for the well-being and development of society. These functions are summarized in the Table that follows.

Forest Functions

For the Natural System	For the Social System
Protective	
− soil protection by absorption and deflection, radiation, precipitation and wind	− sheltering agricultural crops against drought, wind, cold, radiation
− conservation of humidity and carbon dioxide by decreasing wind velocity	− conserving soil and water
− sheltering and providing required conditions for plant and animal species	− shielding man against nuisances (noise, sights, smells, fumes)
Regulative	
− absorption, storage and release of CO_2, O_2 and mineral elements	− improvement of atmospheric conditions in residential and recreational areas
− absorption of aerosols and sound	− improvement of temperature regimes in residential areas (roadside trees, parks)
− absorption, storage and release of water	− improvement of the biotope value and amenity of landscapes

- absorption and transformation of radiant and thermal energy

Productive

- efficient storage of energy in utilizable form in phyto- and zoomass

- supply of a wide array of raw materials to meet man's growing demands

- self-regulating and regenerative processes of wood, bark, fruit and leaf production

- source of employment

- production of a wide array of chemical compounds, such as resins, alcaloids, essential oils, latex, pharmaceuticals, etc.

- creation of wealth

In the case of tropical forests the first two functions – protective and regulative – are extremely important and not very well-known while the third – productive – is largely underestimated and underused.

Tropical Moist Forests as a Genetic Reservoir

Tropical moist forests are of great ecological value. The ecology of tropical moist forests is distinguished by two characteristics: an exceptionally high rate of vegetation growth and an exceptional biological diversity (Jordan 1982). The richness of these forests in terms of the number of species they contain is one of the main reasons why they have attracted particular attention, and why many people feel that their protection is of paramount importance. Scientific research has shown that the study of a single hectare of moist forest reveals the existence of many species hitherto unknown to modern science. We know of some cases where forest species – particularly mammals and birds – have become entirely extinct because of disruption of their habitat. But we can also be quite sure that many species as yet unknown are also becoming extinct as the area of forest declines. Indirectly, this is a matter of considerable humanitarian concern.

In the past, species discovered in the forest have provided the source of many medicines and crops of great value to the human race. Destruction of these forests is undoubtedly against the interests of future generations.[3] To quantify this: it has been estimated that tropical forests contain 50% of all world species. Amazonia alone has one million animal and plant species, 1,800 bird species, 2,000 fish species (four times more than the Zaire basin, eight times more than the Mississippi basin and 10 times more than the whole of Europe). Only 1% have been studied from the point of view of their economic use. The area is indeed the world's largest genetic reservoir.

If a small area inside the forest is cleared and allowed to regenerate naturally, the species composition of the secondary forest should eventually return to normal, as different species invade in turn from the surrounding forest. But when very large areas are cleared or damaged, or when deforestation takes place at the edge of the forest, propagation becomes more difficult for the forest species and the area will tend to have a permanently weakened species structure even if left to regenerate naturally.

Soil deterioration is a second factor which will often prevent regeneration of tropical moist forest. Most soils under tropical moist forest are shallow, and their nutrient availability is low. When forest is cleared, exposure to sunlight, wind, water and other factors such as the impact of the wheels of logging machines destroy soil structure, leading to erosion. Soil deterioration and the difficulties of regeneration of key plant species together mean that the destruction of tropical moist forest is in many cases virtually irreversible, hence the considerable loss of genetic varieties.

Tropical Forests and World Climatic Regulation

Tropical moist forests are of great significance for global, regional and local climate regulation. The contribution of deforestation to the 'greenhouse effect' is probably modest in the short run although this is a controversial issue.[4] But deforestation in moist areas may well be reducing or disturbing rainfall, preventing forest regeneration and having an impact on local and more distant climatic variations which is difficult to assess.

The forest constantly returns water vapour to the air and by shading the soil helps it retain its moisture. In tropical areas, radiation at the earth surface is very high.

This is due to low reflectivity (5-10% below other areas), the fact that the sun is closer to the zenith, and the low temperature of the canopy. Tropical moist forests are therefore efficient absorbers of solar energy which is used in water conversion.

In general, forests return rainfall to the atmosphere in greater proportion than any other vegetative cover. Forests evaporate 50-90% of received rain, whereas grassland returns 40% and bare soil only 30% (Reifsnyder, 1982). Precipitations in the tropical belt are more than three times the world average of 746 mm.

The average surface run-off in tropical areas in 879 mm compared to the world average of 266 mm. Three tropical rivers alone — the Amazon, the Orinoco and the Congo — carry 23% of all surface-water run-off. The Amazon and its tributaries contain two-thirds of all the river waters of the world and 20% of the world fresh water area. But this represents less than 50% of the precipitation in the area: in other words, the evaporation in tropical areas is so high that tropical land surface contributes 62% of the world water vapour. The tropical regions (land surface plus sea surface) which represent 40% of total earth surface contribute 58% of the total volume of vapour. This vapour is transported to the atmosphere outside the tropics as latent heat and plays an important role in the world thermodynamic system.

The 'roughness' of the forest surface, caused by irregularities in the forest canopy and by emergent high trees, slows down the movement of air masses and causes turbulence. This leads to ascending air fluxes, air cooling, cloud formation and, consequently, greater precipitation. It is possible that 20% more rain falls on forests than on any other vegetation (Shiklomanov and Krestovsky, 1984). In Amazonia it is common to see great pillars of cumulus clouds appearing to rise from the top of the forest, and less cloud where the trees thin out.

This influence of tropical forests on climate is generally agreed, but many contradictions and gaps in knowledge remain as regards the relationship between the clearance of tropical forest lands and local climate. If deforestation leads to a reduction in water returned to the atmosphere, it is likely that the effects vary according to the size of the area cleared. There will be little measurable effect within one small area, such as that cleared by a slash-and-burn agriculturalist. The decrease in moisture return may not result in detectably drier atmosphere because of swamping by moist air from surrounding forest. But the effect of many small clearings could be cumulatively very large (Salati et al, 1983).

A possible effect of the clearing of large areas of forest (greater than 100 km^2) would be the increase of the albedo and consequently a reduction in rainfall.[5] A 0.1% increase in albedo can cause a 23% decrease in precipitation. The reduction in rainfall immediately downwind, if focused, could result in a complete change in the structure of the adjacent forest. Essentially such deforestation would trigger a process that would slowly but continuously eat away at forest downwind. Regrowth of vegetation on a small area of clearance can restore the climatological balance within 10-20 years. But again, as with biological diversity, it is unlikely that forest regrowth after large-scale deforestation would achieve this effect.

Types of Forest Conversion

Forest conversion has been a normal feature of development which will not be avoided in tropical areas. But it is important that such a transformation should not disrupt the role that each specific ecosystem plays in the normal functioning of the natural environment. Moreover people living in those areas should remain able to satisfy their needs and the complete process of development should not be jeopardized. The transition should follow certain principles and specific limits. The conversion of tropical forests, in particular, brings about changes in the natural environment which can be beneficial, yet too frequently damage human interests.

Recent concern is focused on over-exploitation of the natural resources, biological productivity and the destruction of the natural environment. The natural ecosystem is disrupted. FAO reports use the term deforestation in the strict sense of complete clearance of tree formations and the conversion of tropical land to other uses. Man-made disturbance ranges from minor quantitative changes to fundamental qualitative and quantitative transformation.

In theory, forests can regenerate within a reasonable period provided there is no permanent loss of biological potential. But rapid destruction of the forest affects its biological potential as well as its protective and regulative capacity and its role as a source of raw materials and other products.

Whether conversion can be achieved without disruption and depletion will depend on forest land-use patterns and on the scale of the process. One of the most ancient agricultural uses of forest land is shifting cultivation or swidden agriculture. Essentially this starts with the rather incomplete clearance of a small area, the burning of the debris and the cultivation of the land for a few years (normally five). Then the land is left and reverts to the state of a secondary forest before it is cleared again. The impact of shifting cultivation varies considerably depending on the type of forest cleared, the fallow period, and population pressure. If the period of cultivation is short and the fallow period rather long, the practice can be regarded as ecologically sound. Soil fertility is renewed and the forest recovers. If not, the original forest will recover only partially or not at all. Where the full recovery of fertility and vegetation is not possible, the land is covered by grass and shrubs. Deterioration becomes permanent. The tropical forest turns into grassland or savanna, and gradually cattle grazing replaces shifting cultivation as a form of land use.

Recently the agricultural use of tropical forest has been accelerated by the influx of peasants following the opening up of forests by logging contractors and highway construction. These migrants know little about tropical forest land. They establish subsistence farming which has little to do with shifting agriculture; they deplete the soil and tend to abandon the area when productivity has fallen.

The felling of trees has been encouraged by the increasing international demand for tropical hardwood. Demand in industrial countries today is 14 to 16 times greater than in 1950, yet the tropical moist forests contribute little more than one-tenth of the current world consumption of wood for construction, pulp and paper and industrial uses.

According to FAO, between 1958 and 1978 about one million square kilometres of forests (385,000 square miles) were leased for tropical timber extraction mainly in South East Asia and West Africa. The great potential of tropical forests is ignored and irreversible damage is often caused to the remaining species in the forest. There are about 2,500 tree species in Amazonia of which only 400 have been assessed for economic purposes. Not more than 50 are exploited. Out of 150 trees per acre, only 6 or 8 are used, but because of inadequate or even predatory logging techniques, the remaining trees and the soil are severely damaged. Selective logging in South East Asia reportedly damages between one- and two-thirds of unused species. One-third of the logged forest soil is left bare and the heavy logging equipment causes severe soil compaction. Some 11,000 square miles of tropical forests are converted every year for commercial timber.

In addition, it has been argued that today the greatest threat to tropical forests is the increasing area devoted to cattle ranching and savanna-type vegetation which preclude forest regeneration. Intensive grazing rapidly weakens a soil ill-suited to this type of use. This kind of conversion is particularly important in Central America and Amazonia in order to supply lower grade meat to the very large North American market (mainly for fast food and pet food). It is reported that since 1950 the pasture area in Central America has doubled at the expense of tropical forests. 38% of deforestation in Brazil between 1966 and 1975 is said to have been caused by ranching.

Road and highway construction is one of the irreversible types of forest conversion which has the additional effect of opening the forest to new uses and facilitating contacts with previously isolated forest dwellers. This kind of deforestation is particularly important in Brazil whose ambitious highway programme between 1966 and 1977 accounted for 25% of Amazonian deforestation.

Industrial agriculture is another type of conversion too frequently ignored. Oil palm and rubber are among the main commodities produced for the international markets.

Finally, minor types of conversion are associated with forest clearing due to mining and hydro-electric schemes.

Six Humanitarian Situations

Six situations require close scrutiny from the humanitarian point of view both because of short-term and long-term effects of forest clearing:

(1) Situations where an extraordinary and untapped biological wealth with enormous potential for social development is seriously threatened;

(2) Situations where extensive forms of agricultural or pastoral land-use threaten to diminish the long-term suitability of the land for cultivation or forestry;

(3) Situations where forest loss may jeopardize climatic balance at local, regional and global levels and trigger a cumulative deterioration in ecological potential;

(4) Situations where forest clearing activities and/or an influx of population involve a sudden transformation of land-use;

(5) Situations where the survival of indigenous dwellers is threatened by deforestation;

(6) Situations of increasing malnutrition and ill-health.

Notes

1. These are the regional estimates presented by Lanly in FAO (1982). They are figures for deforestation of closed forest areas; percentages for deforestation of all forest (closed and open) are slightly lower. These estimates correspond to a fairly narrow definition of deforestation, and do not include many more or less severe kinds of forest degradation. As a general rule, positive transformation to completely different, and valuable, forms of land-use is classed as deforestation; much of the real problem thus lies in degradation rather than outright deforestation.

2. A good example is the case of Sierra Leone, one of the few African countries where forest cover is no longer declining, but only because hardly any forest remains! Two hundred years ago the country had a high forest cover of 75%. Ruthless exploitation, mainly for the British market, helped to reduce this area to a mere 3%, spread over the country in remnants of negligible size. The only remaining forest which still merits the name is the Gola Forest, on the Liberian border. Now, with German development aid financing a saw-mill, this last pocket will disappear within the coming years.

3. Loss of species has been discussed by Myers (1980), R. and C. Prescott-Allen (1983), the U.S. Department of State (1982) and others. There is also a substantial economic literature discussing the inter-generational equity problem presented by species loss. The welfare of future generations is an important humanitarian issue which this paper has not sought to address in detail.

4. NAS (1983) illustrates a growing consensus that, although deforestation (and more generally use of fire in forest areas) has contributed to a CO_2 build-up, this contribution is less critical than fossil fuel combustion. For a somewhat different view, cf. Myers (1982).

5. Albedo: the ratio of solar radiation which is returned to the atmosphere. The albedo of a well-developed forest is 0.1, that of a desert 0.4.

3. Towards Sound Forest Management

In Chapter 1 we described some of the problems of people living on tropical forest lands: disease, malnutrition, and physical insecurity. Chapter 2 examined the relevance of tropical forests for mankind as a genetic reservoir and as a climatic regulator and reviewed the main types of forest conversion and their importance. We shall now consider whether sound forest management is feasible.

'Runway' and 'Treadmill' Deforestation

There is often a fine balance between the costs and benefits of forest development. The forest is a form of economic capital, passed on from generation to generation. Traditional forest development seeks to use that capital, and to transform it for other productive uses. Forests become pastures and farmland; timber fuels industrial ovens and makes saw-mills turn. Yet no action is taken for the *reproduction*, let alone the expansion, of this form of capital.

Some countries have engaged in *runway deforestation:* they have tried to achieve 'take-off' into modern industrial society by turning natural forest capital into agricultural and industrial wealth. In Ivory Coast, timber has been the largest foreign exchange earner, and the country has been the largest African timber exporter. At the same time, for every cubic metre of wood extracted by the Ivorian timber industry, 4.5 cubic metres have been destroyed by agricultural clearance. Of 12 million hectares of closed forest only some 2 million now remain. The timber industry is now declining in importance as reserves of more valuable timber species are exhausted. Ivory Coast is not without its share of forest development problems: the dry season often brings damaging fires in the cash-crop plantations of the forest zone, and recent droughts have dried up reservoirs and led to cuts in electricity supply.

In many developing countries, the forest has been exploited and degraded to fulfil the needs of immediate consumption. These countries are engaged in a process of *treadmill deforestation*: forest capital is being eaten up just to prevent economies from slipping backwards. In countries as varied as Nepal, Uganda, Ghana and Zaire, forest capital is liquidated and yet per capita incomes continue to fall.

Only political will can ensure that people stay with the land they have, benefiting from a nation's financial and administrative resources to make the land productive — productive this year, productive the next, and still productive into the future, a truly sustainable natural resource base.

Deforestation is a humanitarian problem which traditional forest clearing has done much to create and little to solve. To meet people's needs in tropical forest lands, we must learn to put aside questions of short-term economic profitability and accept that, in the end, ensuring a sustainable natural resource base is an objective in itself and a condition for sustainable development.

Realistically, it must be accepted that deforestation and ecological degradation will continue in the tropics. In order to reduce the pace of deforestation, to make the forest conversion less harmful to the long-term prospects of human civilization in the tropical environment, efforts should be made to ensure that conversion is the vehicle of sustainable development; and, at the same time, ensure that forest areas of particular socio-economic or ecological value are preserved.

Environmental Management for Major Forest Development Projects

Deforestation is caused less by forestry operations than by roads, dams, ranching and resettlement programmes and other work carried out by government departments and transnational corporations that have no direct responsibility for forest conservation or forestry production. Many of these programmes are financed by capital at near-market rates lent by the major international development banks. In the forestry sector, the World Bank, for example, makes commitments of less than $100 million per year globally. Yet in a single country the Bank may commit more than this on one major development project alone.

We have said that, in forestry, one cannot always be sure of achieving the best results by pursuing the highest rate of return. Yet the international development banks must obtain much of their finance on commercial markets. On the whole, however, these banks are in a position to borrow and lend at slightly less than market rates of interest; the World Bank, in particular, is sometimes in a position to make a judicious mixture of hard loans from the IBRD and soft loans from IDA.[1] It is critically important that these banks and their clients use all opportunities available to incorporate into projects elements of environmental management and social development for the populations affected by the project. Even relatively small components of this type can make much difference to a project's impact on the long-term potential of the area, long after loans are repaid and equipment amortized.

Part of the wealth generated by a major project must be returned immediately to the area to enable careful management of the disturbed forest site. In appraising the Polonoroeste Project in Brazil, the World Bank remarked that severe problems of environmental degradation, social inequality and lawlessness were likely to arise during implementation, but felt that without its participation the area's prospects would be grimmer still. This is not an image of their work that development finance institutions like to promote, but it is very real nevertheless. It should be recognized that preventing environmental damage is one of the most important roles of the international development finance community today.

The experience – and it is valuable experience – that these development institutions have accumulated has often been an experience of failure: of the severe environmental damage done by otherwise successful projects and of projects which have failed through inadequate attention to environmental and social side-effects. This experience needs to be shared, frankly and without complacency, with developing countries who have a right to learn from past mistakes.

Total Protection of Exceptional Sites

Total protection of tropical forest is only justifiable when this does not involve substantial privation for local populations. But there are still many areas where total protection is justified. Such ecological protection, which will bear no short-term economic returns, provides two important humanitarian benefits: it protects resources for the populations of the future; and it provides an opportunity to cater for the needs of indigenous groups living in harmony with the forest. The Biosphere Reserve concept of the UNESCO *Man and the Biosphere* Programme is one of several schemes which explicitly cater for the needs of indigenous groups, regarding them as part of the protected ecological system and not as hostile to it. But adequate environmental management, financial and political support, and constant monitoring are essential.

Focal Programmes for Areas of High Stress

A number of areas of tropical forest land are affected by accelerated environmental degradation as a result of excessive deforestation. These areas include countries where per capita income has fallen over a period of more than 20 years, as in Ghana, Uganda and Nepal (World Bank, 1984). The West African case is of particular importance, since there is a growing suspicion that deforestation in the forest zone may interact with desertification in the arid and semi-arid zones to amplify climatic disturbance.[2]

In singling out Sub-Saharan Africa as an area in urgent need of increased assistance, the World Bank coined the term 'accelerated development'. It is difficult for many people to understand what an acceleration of development can entail in an area where per capita GNP fell overall throughout the 1970s or why an increase in development assistance is necessarily an appropriate response (Eicher, 1982). It is unfortunate that greater emphasis was not placed on the role of environmental management in a focal programme of this kind.

It is widely recognized that changes in economic incentives and structures of land tenure may do more to help areas of high stress than the injection of large amounts of assistance. Yet in tropical forest areas such as West Africa, the eastern Himalayan watersheds and the Pacific Andean coast where natural disasters such as fire, flood and drought are known to be exacerbated by deforestation, generous financial support is required for environmental management. With care, this is a field where assistance can make a major contribution with comparatively little likelihood of exacerbating structural problems in the local economy. Furthermore, such programmes can provide great benefits at relatively low cost.

Ensuring Careful Forest Clearance

Clearance and fire − for slash-and-burn agriculture − are two essential tools of people living in tropical forest and savanna. They have been used since time immemorial; their scientific justification for agricultural and pastoral yield improvement is well-documented; they are frequently ingrained in social tradition and custom. They may change, but they need not harm the environment.

Improperly used, or used by a growing population experiencing an increasingly acute conflict over use and control of land, fire and clearance are powerful and dangerous tools indeed. Pre-emptive clearance of forest can undermine the basis for a rational and equitable allocation of land uses. Fire can be used directly as an offensive weapon in the ejection and expropriation of local cultivators.[3] The uses of tradition may become the misuses of a changing present. There are an increasing number of cases where migrating or expanding groups come into conflict with other social groups over use and occupation of tropical lands.

Fire and heavy machinery used by international corporations to clear tropical forest and convert them into ranching areas inflict the worst damage. Many national governments have sought to impose laws on fire clearance. These laws have frequently been seen as an attempt to alienate land from its natural occupants, and the legal approach has proved largely ineffectual in many cases. Governments themselves are often responsible for damage in forest clearance, as when manual clearance techniques are replaced by heavy machinery which compacts and erodes the soil.[4] National governments continue to have a responsibility to find ways of helping rural people to exercise proper care in clearance. There is a considerable fund of scientific and technical knowledge available for controlling their use. It has been more difficult for governments to control the clearing activities of international corporations.

There are great disparities between the land areas available for rural households in different tropical forest lands. In South East Africa, 2-4 hectares has become a typical plot for one household to cultivate and manage. In much of Latin America, 50-200 hectares is the norm on pioneer colonization fronts: when they fail, these smallholdings are often replaced by huge ranches. One of the main targets of research on tropical husbandry should be to discover the best methods of sustainable exploitation that can be employed on farms of standard size under different conditions. If it can be demonstrated that a fifty-hectare plot of forest in Latin America can be managed through a mixture of gathering and gardening techniques to provide a livelihood for one household, it may be possible to turn the tide on unsustainable, extensive forms of land-use.[5]

At present, much of the latent conflict over land-use is dissipated by further forest clearance: there is still enough to go round. Reports of violence and forcible expropriation, particularly in Central America but also in areas such as Uganda and Assam, are not necessarily signs of lawlessness and a breakdown of social structures; they are in many cases signs of a simple, physical lack of land. The search for production systems which use less land and use it sustainably can make a major contribution to defusing such conflicts.

Forest Management and National Planning

This report has referred to the experience of many different people and places throughout the tropics. The problems of forest development must be solved at the local level, by people who understand them in detail, as they affect each community.

Mistakes in national planning have a profound influence on the lives of many forest people. Credit facilities are a typical example. Poor, landless peasants in many countries depend on sources of credit for any chance of improving their lot. Yet credit institutions put conditions on credit which often deprive it of all usefulness. They require proof of title to land as loan security – but many peasants have never had a legal title and have no means of acquiring it. They grant credit for stocking cattle on smallholdings vulnerable to leaching and erosion. They restrict the choice of agricultural crops, lending for rice production when cassava gives higher and more regular yields. They give preference to loans for mature forest clearance, encouraging wasteful deforestation.

The pressure originating outside tropical forest areas should be assessed and controlled. It is caused by international demand for cheap meat and hardwood and also by national boundaries and peasant immigration. This process of migration reflects population pressure not in the forest itself but in other areas. It is therefore essential to include forest development in the overall development process.

These and many other cases of mistaken planning decisions are reported in all parts of the tropics. They often stem from two basic weaknesses in land-use planning. The closed forest is treated as a free and permanent/renewable source of raw materials: forest plans in national planning concentrate on trade in timber, and ignore the fact that the forest provides a habitat to many people. And deforested or degraded areas are treated as if the forest has no role to play in socio-economic development, when these areas above all need forestry management and care. To bring natural resource management into planning is to match national decisions to the needs of people, for these natural resources are the base on which the poor of forest lands must live.

Notes

1. IDA finance is of course normally extended to low-income countries only.

2. Cf. Arnaud and Sournia (1980). This subject is still imperfectly understood, but it is widely felt that it would be most unwise to await detailed scientific confirmation before envisaging remedial action.

3. A striking case has been documented in the region of Santarem in Para State, Brazil, by Bonkers (1982).

4. Combinations of manual and mechanical clearance techniques may often be the most economic. Government projects are often also responsible for waste of considerable valuable timber (cf. Ross & Donovan 1984).

5. Research is currently being conducted by Dr J. Clay on behalf of UNESCO on this subject.

4. Deforestation and Human Health

The settling of a group of colonists, road builders, cattle ranchers, or loggers, brings about many changes in the forest. Large tracts are cut by newly arrived colonists, often more than is necessary for the maintenance of their families. Hunting and destruction of habitats by deforestation decreases the numbers of forest-dependent animals and causes beasts of prey to retreat. The only animals favoured are rodents which proliferate unhindered, causing damage to crops and property, while providing more food for hematophagous insects. Shrinking bird and bat populations enhance the expansion of insect populations.

Deep tracks and ruts cut by heavy vehicles and the puddles which arise everywhere where there is stagnation in drainage provide excellent breeding sites for insects. Even the water left behind by the rain in a discarded tyre or car can sustain a whole population of malaria mosquitoes. This disturbed environment, the introduction of new diseases by travellers and colonists, and the increasing numbers of rodents and insects can change a relatively healthy forest area within a few years into a disease-ridden hell.

Although quite a number of diseases are in fact forest borne, they normally do not afflict human populations in a serious way unless ecological disturbance takes place.

Disturbed Environment and Disease

Diseases present in the undisturbed forest may not constitute a threat as man may not be the prime host, or the vector may live in the higher strata of the forest so that it would not normally meet a potential human victim. But, as soon as the preferred host animals disappear or as the stratification of the forest is altered, a disease may suddenly break out.

Leishmaniasis

The parasitical disease American leishmaniasis, a disease normally only acquired by those penetrating natural forests, occurs in different forms which cause a range of severe and incurable skin lesions in humans and can be fatal. The infection is caused by a protozoal parasite and is transferred by sandflies. The normal natural hosts of the disease are several species of forest animals, such as sloths, anteaters and rats, between which parasites and sandflies circulate. When the forest is entered or disturbed by man the sandfly can turn itself on this new host. In Central America the disease is known as *chiclero's ulcer*. The *chicleros*, as their name implies, are the men who collect the 'chicle' or chewing gum from the sapodilla tree, for which purpose they spend up to six months of the year living in the forest. As this period coincides with the rainy season, and therefore with maximum sandfly density, it is not surprising that there has always been a high infection rate among the *chicleros*. The reservoir of infection is found among forest rodents in which the parasite also causes skin lesions.

Nowadays, the disease is more and more common, throughout Latin America, in people who are actively involved with deforestation: miners, colonists, loggers, road construction teams. Since forest destruction actually favours some of the animal hosts such as rats and opossums, the disease can easily spread. This happened, for example, near Manaus (Brazil) in a newly developed housing area, surrounded by high forest, where an increasing number of leishmaniasis cases in human beings were being reported. It appeared that 60-70% of the opossums caught in this area were infected. It was suggested that this very high infection rate resulted from the withdrawal of the primary hosts (such as sloths and anteaters) due to man's disturbance and an increase in the opossum population because these animals are scavengers by nature and are attracted by man's presence. In undisturbed natural forests, opossums are rarely found infected since they do not concentrate and therefore are only rarely exposed to the sandfly vector (Lainson, 1983).

The habits of the different sandfly species are a limiting factor in the spread of the disease. Scientific research has proved that there exists a much greater number of different leishmaniasis parasites in sylvatic animals, which until now do not affect man, only because the transmitting sandfly species does not feed on humans. Some cases of new forms of leishmaniasis in the Brazilian Amazon are attributed to 'errors' of the sandfly vector. Introduction of a better-adapted vector along the newly constructed highways or a change of taste in the actual vector might cause new and unexpected outbreaks of leishmaniasis.

Chagas' Disease

A forest-borne disease which is often freely carried into houses is the sleeping-sickness related Chagas' disease. In Venezuela it was discovered that the traditional use of palm thatch for roofs often carries the eggs of the Chagas' disease vector, a bug, into the houses. The eggs, which stick to the palm fronds, appeared to be a major source of infection of this illness. Replacement of palm thatch with corrugated metal roofs has been a major factor in controlling the Chagas vector bug in Venezuela (Schofield and White, 1983).

As with leishmaniasis, there are a number of vector bug species which can be a potential threat to people penetrating the forest. Since 1969, seven cases of an unknown variety of Chagas' disease have been reported, transmitted by a non-domiciliated bug. Introduction of an already domiciliated vector bug might cause an accelerated spread of this new disease (Lainson, 1979).

The house sparrow, by carrying the vector in its feathers, has been implicated in spreading Chagas' disease northward in Brazil — it spread 1,500 km up the Brasilia-Belém highway in six years and has already advanced beyond Maraba (Goodland, 1975).

Malaria

Possibly the most serious disease of the tropics, malaria, is present in every area being deforested. Globally there are some 5 million new cases per year of this mosquito-spread disease, with one million African children dying of it annually. A total of 1.2 billion people live in risk areas. The disease is spreading after recent major resurgence, although WHO has carried out intensive eradication campaigns which have been successful in some areas in Asia and Latin America. The disease is most often carried and spread by travellers or migrants; this has contributed to its resurgence in Northern Brazil and in Nepal. Infected agricultural colonists are major carriers. With their forestry activities they clearly extend the geographic limits of malaria.

In Paraguay it was found that the productivity of farmers engaged in slash-and-burn agriculture can be severely curbed by malaria, and, most strikingly, that the most affected families were always relative newcomers to the region. The extra effort which they had to spend on clearing forests for crops was high, because when they took up residence there were only very small portions, if any, cleared for crops. It is possible that this extra workload made these farmers more vulnerable to malaria. Harvesting normally coincides with the malaria season, but due to illness from malaria, productivity could decrease by 25%, affecting their economic as well as their nutritional position (Conly, 1975).

Although the ecology of the different malaria transmitters, the *Anopheles* mosquitoes, can differ significantly, there are a number of them which only live in a forest environment. One of the malaria vectors in South East Asia, *anopheles balbacensis*, proliferates especially in half-shaded pools, a habitat which is found particularly in selectively logged forests and along forest streams and rivers. Research has proved that elimination of the mosquito is best achieved by clearing forest along suspected streams and pools. Clear felling, however, normally conflicts with sound forest management in the tropics and can, especially on riverbanks, accelerate erosion. Moreover the wheels of extraction equipment may inadvertently create additional breeding sites. *Anopheles balbacensis* only starts feeding after midnight and its flight range is normally not more than 500 m. Dr G.B. White of the London School of Hygiene and Tropical Medicine therefore suggests that dwellings be situated at least 1 km away from the forest fringe, while people such as loggers and hunters should use bednets when staying overnight in the forests. Focal spraying is especially recommended in situations such as in Thailand where development programmes require villages to be surrounded by forests and plantations in which these vectors are likely to thrive.

Two diseases, malaria and scrub typhus, also have a relationship with the establishment of plantations, where they represent a major health hazard to the human population in modern development schemes. In 1911, during the establishment of the first rubber plantations in Malaysia, it was reported that 9,000 out of the total estate labour force of 143,000 died from malaria. Some estates had a mortality rate of 20% every year in the pioneering phase. In 1958, eradication campaigns successfully reduced malaria admission to hospitals to 0.095% of the population. But this considerable improvement has not been sustained in rural areas. In 1974, it was observed that in new settlements the incidence of malaria yielded 100 cases a month in 2,000 households, with almost every household having at least one sufferer. The vector, *anopheles maculatus*, is particularly associated with the slower flowing sections of sunlit streams, a habitat which is easily created during felling for a plantation. Conditions become unfavourable for the insect as soon as the plantation shades out the stream again (Edington and Edington, unpublished).

Scrub Typhus
Scrub typhus is propagated in the imperata grass which appears in the process of savannization after the clearing of a tropical forest. The picture which emerges is similar to the transmission of malaria. From observations made in Malaysia in 1975 at a rural health centre serving an oil

plantation scheme, it was estimated that there were about 400 cases of scrub typhus annually among the 10,000 settlers. Extrapolated to West Malaysia as a whole, this would give a figure of 500,000 people affected. Since the complicated ecological background of the disease has not been fully appreciated by every leader of development projects, the disease is still likely to thrive. The main point of attack are chiggers which normally feed on the Malayan wood rat, a rodent living high in the palm canopy. A young, recently established oil palm plantation brings host, vector and man in a dangerous juxtaposition for the transmission of scrub typhus. The risks appear to diminish towards the end of the first decade of the plantation when the canopy of the palm trees is high and closer.

These findings have direct relevance to human health and to Malaysia's land development programme, in which the establishment of new oil plantations is playing such an essential role. Both malaria and scrub typhus are an extra burden on the independent farmers who are obliged to make regular loan payments once their crop has started to yield. The loss of working time due to illness only adds to this pressure.

Schistosomiasis
Some tropical diseases are directly related to a changing use of the environment. One case is the spreading of schistosomiasis in Amazonia. Since the natural conditions of the waters in Amazonia are inimical to the spread of the disease, nearly all water being acid and oligotrophic, there was no great danger of the disease spreading. This situation, however, is now coming to an end, as colonists throughout Amazonia are encouraged by agricultural agencies to use lime and fertilizer on their fields. The poor quality of the soil combined with heavy rains soon leaches all these nutrients into ditches and, subsequently, rivers. The resulting autrophication and rise of alkalinity, together with the general increase in agricultural settlements and colonies, causes very favourable conditions for snail vectors to thrive.

The continuous influx of settlers out of the already infected region of north-eastern Brazil poses an increasing threat to the entire area. Control of the snail and of the infection is possible, but requires measures combining strict sanitation with application of chemicals. Worldwide, throughout the tropics, 180 million people carry the disease, with these numbers still increasing.

Deforestation and Trypanosomiasis

The tse-tse fly is the vector of the greatly feared African trypanosomiasis, which affects both humans and cattle (the human form is also known as sleeping sickness). It is practically impossible to raise cattle in an area where try-panosomiasis is endemic. An indication of how much the disease is feared is shown by the observation that a single tse-tse inside a car is a common cause of road accidents due to panic among the passengers and distraction of the driver (World Bank, 1980). It is claimed that if the tse-tse fly were not present, the whole of the African tropical forest area could be converted to cattle ranching for export meat production. The factors inhibiting this development are discussed below.

The vector has a complicated ecology. The tse-tse fly transmits the trypanosomes to wild animals, cattle and man. For its survival the fly depends on bush or humid areas where it breeds and rests. The flies are most danger-ous near the hot dry limit of their range, because they tend to gather along springs and pools, where the chance of contact with humans is very high. Even a small plot of forest left in an otherwise tree-less area, for example a sacred grove, can provide a habitat for the fly. It thrives at its best in the fringes between human settlements and the undisturbed forests, waiting to re-colonize the rest whenever suitable bush-cover offers a new habitat and animals to feed on. This implies that in areas with active deforestation the chance of contracting the disease is very high.

The vulnerability of cattle and man to the disease makes it unattractive to encroach upon this environment. Until now there are only a few breeds of cattle, like the dwarf Dahomey cows, which are trypano-tolerant. This has evolved over thousands of years by natural selection and is almost equal to the tolerance in indigenous wild animals, but Dahomey cattle are much less productive than other breeds. FAO plans to improve matters by breeding a new hybrid cow which combines tolerance with higher meat production. Success in this would make new human expansion into the African rainforests possible. Control of the disease is being pursued in large-scale programmes throughout the African continent. Initially this focused on destroying the flies' habitat by ruthless forest clearing, which proved very successful, particularly in Nigeria. The effects on the vegetation and its dependent fauna, however, were disastrous and can well have serious side-effects on climate and water-flows. Other rigorous measures consisted of killing all wild animal hosts, a solution as radical as clearing the vegetation since these hosts range from rats to rhinoceroses.

Research in Kenya proved that tse-tse flies obtain 50% of their meals from bush-buck, an antelope species which prefers thickets near streams. Infected flies transmit the parasite to the animals during a blood meal. Later on, healthy flies pick up trypanosomes from sick animals and become infected. Man may become part of this cycle by exposure to the fly bite. Normally infection can also be transmitted by a fly which has fed on an infected animal and not an infected person. Control of the animal host can therefore be an important means of control.

Both vegetation clearing and animal killing methods are virtually abandoned today, due to the high costs and the need for follow-up every few years when the vegetation has regrown or the animal population has returned. Modern vector control methods consist mainly of spraying insecticides, focusing on highly suspected resting places. Effective control can be done at high cost (e.g. Zimbabwe) but has proved almost impossible in dense forest areas.

Sprayed areas need periodic treatment since the fly returns as soon as the toxic effect has washed away. Most of the insecticides used are organochlorines, which can well build up in the food chain, eventually affecting man. The most reasonable way to cope with trypanosomiasis is to accept it as part of the ecosystem, in fact as one of its in-built safeguards. The introduction of cattle ranching into the tropical forests of Africa will have serious effects on the soil and on human societies, as can be observed in Latin America. The forest might instead be used for the extraction of bushmeat and other forest products. When this is carried out in a sustainable manner, it avoids risks to cattle and man and can offer natural and long-lasting services to local economies.

Difficulties in Disease Control

There is a strong relationship between the disturbance of tropical forests and the emergence of diseases as described above. The paradoxical fact that some diseases, such as leishmaniasis, are actually best remedied by cutting down the forest completely while other diseases such as scrub typhus only begin to thrive after the forest has been cut, does not make for easy solutions. The highly ingenious mechanisms of disease transmission can cause unpleasant surprises during the development of a forested area. It may suddenly appear that a certain unexpected disease vector, such as the chiggers in the scrub typhus example, poses a serious threat to a development project and the people working on it.

It is very difficult to foresee which specific action in a forest might cause a disease outbreak, firstly because the ecology and epidemiology of many diseases are not completely known and secondly because not all forest-borne diseases are known. Goodland (1975) gives an example of the latter possibility: during work on the Trans-Amazonian Highway, a 'black fever' broke out at Labrea. This highly lethal disease appeared to be a kind of hepatitis, but of a completely unknown etiology. An unknown haemorrhagic fever, allegedly transmitted by the black fly which is also the onchocerciasis vector, has caused two deaths and 92 cases in Altamira.

Presumably there are many more of these undescribed or unknown diseases, particularly those caused by viruses and mycoses. Whether their discovery will result in immediate remedial action depends on the alertness of the responsible health officers rather than on a well-designed strategy for the prevention of diseases.

The Green Frontier

Many of the diseases among people living in areas of deforestation are associated with low standards of living. Settlers and colonists do not normally tend to come and live in tropical forest areas because of their affluence. They are anxious to get started as soon as possible, build their homestead and develop their land, and often do not bother too much about hygiene and sanitation. Household refuse, water left in cans, cattle, poultry, dogs and very provisional sanitary supplies, combined with a disturbed ecological balance, cause many other (not directly forest-borne) diseases to thrive.

Intestinal parasites are common everywhere throughout tropical forest areas. The primitive living conditions and lack of hygiene can cause whole populations to carry certain infections. In Amazonia over 90% of a test group examined carried *Ascaris* parasites and over 50% *Trichuris*. For Amazonia Goodland (1975) also mentions the following diseases which are carried into the area by migrants: diphtheria, poliomyelitis, tetanus and typhoid. All of these are controllable by routine immunization of newcomers. Good health education should cause the awareness necessary to prevent them from becoming more serious.

Tribal People, Health and Deforestation

All large areas with rain forests have their own groups of tribal people, who may have lived there for centuries. As hunter-gatherers or as true shifting cultivators, they roam vast territories in small numbers. By trial and error they have learnt to use the ecosystem of the tropical forest on a truly sustained basis.

Tribal people have always had their own medical treatments to control endemic diseases. But, because of their independent development, out of contact with society at large, they are susceptible to any infectious disease to which they have not previously been exposed, often with fatal consequences. Examples of this are to be found throughout the world, but again the most striking are in

Brazil. In A.D. 1500 there were an estimated six to nine million Amerindians in Brazil. Today barely 200,000 survive — a decline of two million people per century. The total number of tribes dropped from 230 in 1900 to about half that in 1980. This was caused more by disease and starvation than by conflict (Goodland, 1982). Even common and curable infections such as measles or the common cold can have a disastrous effect on tribal people, primarily attacking the children. Protection or isolation is essential until a vaccination campaign can be carried out, both for tribal peoples and settlers.

Deforestation Without Disease?

Some 140 million forest farmers all over the world depend on tropical forests to provide them with new land every two to three years, in remote areas and conditions. They live on the real frontiers of human society, facing nature and urged to open up the forest in order to survive. These frontier conditions do not encourage them to create healthier surroundings as their homestead will always be a temporary one.

Moreover, it is clear that their numbers will not decline in the foreseeable future. The influx of new forest farmers, together with the natural population increase, could well double the number of forest-dependent people by the year 2000. Spears (1983), assuming 100 million people directly dependent on tropical forest for their farm lands, calculates that about 0.6 to 1.0 billion hectares are needed to sustain that population under a shifting cultivation system, i.e. all the remaining area of tropical forest in the entire world. This population will not stabilize at 100 million, so in fact their prospects become grimmer every day. This outlook poses a threat to the forest, but also to the health and welfare of more and more people.

Most of the forest-related diseases described above can be controlled or prevented, provided the government and the settlers are prepared for them. A sensible planning programme for tribal people must give them freedom to adapt at their own speed and also allow time to carry out the necessary vaccination programmes. Many of the diseases are associated with the low standards of living and will disappear if these are improved. However, this is not a simple task with a steadily rising population of rural poor living in the forest fringe.

A settlement programme projected for a forest area should be preceded by a thorough research of the possible diseases present in the area. When these are difficult to control and dangerous to man or his livestock, or when the area contains diseases which will be aggravated by the disturbance of the environment (e.g. leishmaniasis), a change of plan or project area should seriously be considered. This can particularly be the case with a cattle-raising project in tse-tse infested areas. When the soil is too poor to secure the long-term success of the project on the same site, it may well be that the financial and environmental costs of regular residual spraying will not be outweighed by the short-term benefits of the project. In that case the project should be planned in a different area or involve different ways of using the soil.

Encouragement to keep house surroundings clean and a basic education in sanitation, hygiene and nutrition will go far in checking diseases which are directly related to un-hygienic and poor living standards. Sound planning should anticipate the possible constraints of the project site and their consequences for new settlers. The central planning authority, the conservation agency, the ministries of health, resources and agriculture and the implementing local authorities must all recognize their responsibility in this.

Some necessary components of an effective assessment of the project site in a tropical forest and its capacities for development should include:

★ intensive survey for disease vectors and hosts;
★ inventory of drainage patterns;
★ clinical survey of the population in the project area for contagious diseases;
★ direct treatment of cases of vector-borne diseases;
★ spraying of aircraft and vehicles arriving from areas where vector-borne diseases are endemic (e.g. malaria).

A stringent screening of all people entering the area will help prevent the spread of disease. Free and obligatory treatment will prevent uncontrolled spreading of disease and will then protect the local, uninfected population. Extensive immunization programmes for contagious diseases such as diphtheria, tuberculosis, poliomyelitis, tetanus and the typhoids are indispensable.

A project which also involves the provision of housing should comply with the following conditions (World Bank, 1980):

★ adequate sanitary facilities;
★ regular sanitary inspection and enforcement;
★ safe water system;
★ elimination of hiding places for vermin;
★ monitoring of water and food supplies;
★ control of the number of inhabitants.

Those diseases which are forest-borne and increased by ecological disturbance, such as leishmaniasis, malaria and onchocerciasis, should be controlled by environmental management as far as possible. However, if overpopulation or infertile soils lead people to move to a new tract of forest every few years, there is then little chance that these measures will be continuously applied. This demands great effort on the part of the responsible authorities and great awareness on the part of the inhabitants.

A high priority should therefore go to developing safe and sustainable agricultural methods which are adapted to the soil. Planning which involves both social and ecological constraints can provide a safeguard against both diseases and project failure.

Bibliography

AGARWAL, A. and ANAND, A. (1983). 'Ask the Women who do the Work' in *New Scientist*, pp. 302-206, 4 November 1983.

ANON. (1984). 'Effect of Tropical Forest on Water Yield'. Paper presented at U.N. University Workshop on Forests, Climate and Hydrology – Regional Impacts. Oxford.

ARNAUD, J.C. and SOURNIA, G. (1980). 'Les forêts de Côte d'Ivoire' in *Annales de l'Université d'Abidjan*, Serie G-IX, pp. 5-94.

BENDER, D. (1984). 'Delivering Health Care in the Andes' in *Cultural Survival Quarterly*, Vol, 8, No.2, pp. 51-53.

BERGER, T.R. (1977). *Northern Frontier, Northern Homeland: The Report of the Mackenzie Valley Pipeline Inquiry*. Ministry of Supply and Services, Ottawa.

BLACKIE, J.R. (ed.) et al. (1980). *Environmental Effects of Deforestation: An Annotated Bibliography*. Ambleside: Freshwater Biological Association Occasional Publication No. 10.

74

BOERBOOM, J.H.A. and WIERSUM, K.F. (1983). 'Human Impact on Tropical Moist Forest' in Holzner, W. et al (eds.) *Man's Impact on Vegetation*. The Hague, pp. 83-106.

BRAATZ, S. and DEWEES, P. (1984). *Wood that the People Plant: The Changing Profile of Forestry Assistance*. International Institute for Environment and Development, Washington, D.C. (unpublished).

BREMER J. et al (1984). *Fragile Lands*, a theme paper on problems, issues and approaches for development of humid tropical lowlands and steep slopes in the Latin American region. Washington, D.C., Development Alternatives, Inc.

BROWN, L.R. (1984). *State of the World in 1984; Progress Towards a Sustainable Society*. New York, Worldwatch Institute.

CASSELS, D., HAMILTON, L.S. and SAPLACO, S.R. (1982). *Understanding the Role of Forests in Watershed Protection*. Honolulu, East-West Center.

CAUFIELD, C. (1982). *Tropical Moist Forest: The Resource, the People, the Threats*. London, Earthscan Press Briefing Document No. 32.

CAUFIELD, C. (1984). 'Indonesia's Great Exodus', *New Scientist*, 17 May 1984, London.

CECELSKI, E. (1984). 'The Rural Energy Crisis, Women's Work and Family Welfare: Perspectives and Approaches to Action', *World Employment Programme Research Working Paper,* ILO, Geneva (unpublished).

CHASE-SMITH, R. (1982). 'The Dialectics of Domination in Peru: Native Communities and the Myth of the Vast Amazonian Emptiness', *Cultural Survival,* Occasional Paper No. 8.

CONLY, G.N. (1975). *The Impact of Malaria on Economic Development: a Case Study.* Washington, D.C., Pan American Health Organization, Sc. Publ. No. 297.

CULTURAL SURVIVAL (1979). *Special Report – Brazil.*

CULTURAL SURVIVAL (1984). 'Women in a Changing World', *Cultural Survival Quarterly,* Vol. 8, No. 2.

DORFMAN, A. (1984). 'Bread and Burnt Rice: Culture and Economic Survival in Latin America' in *Grassroots Development,* Vol. 8, No. 2.

EDINGTON, J.M. & M.A. 'Ecology and Rural Development in West Malaysia'. University College, Cardiff (unpublished).

EEC (1982). 'Food Strategies — A New Form of Co-operation between Europe and Countries of the Third World' in *European Information — Development,* Brussels.

EICHER, C.K. (1982). 'Facing Up to Africa's Fuel Crisis' in *Foreign Affairs,* Vol. 61, No. 1.

FRANZEN VINADE, L.F. et al (1980). 'Causas do desmatamento em pequenas propriedades no municipio de Frederico Westphalen', *Revista do Centro de Ciencias Rurais,* 10(3).

GARZON, C.E. (1984). *Water Quality in Hydro-Electric Projects,* Washington, D.C., World Bank.

GHEE, L.T. (1977). *Peasants and their Agricultural Economy in Colonial Malaya 1874-1941.* OUP, Kuala Lumpur.

GJORDING, C.N. (1981). 'The Cerro Colorado Copper Project and the Guaymi Indians of Panama', *Cultural Survival,* Occasional Paper No. 3.

GOODLAND, Robert. (1982). *Tribal Peoples and Economic Development*, World Bank, Washington, D.C.

GUPPY, N. (1984). 'Tropical Deforestation: A Global View'. *Foreign Affairs*, Vol. 62, No. 4, pp. 928-965.

HARRISON, P. (1983). 'Land and People, the Growing Pressure'. *Earthwatch*, No. 13.

HARRISON, P. and ROWLEY J. (1984), *Human Numbers, Human Needs*. London, International Planned Parenthood Federation.

HENDERSON-SELLERS, A. (1981). 'Climate sensitivity variations in vegetated landsurface albedoa' in *roc. Annual Climate Diagn. Workshop,* Columbia University, pp. 135-144.

HOUGHTON, D. and MOORE, B. (1984). 'The effects of human interference with the natural cycle of carbon by burning fossil fuels, harvesting forests.' Paper presented at the UN University Workshop on Forests, Climate and Hydrology – Regional Impacts, Oxford.

HUDSON, J.E. (1984). 'The *Anopheles darlingii* problem in the Surinam Rain Forest' in *Bulletin of Entomological Research,* London.

INTER-AMERICAN COMMISSION ON HUMAN RIGHTS (1982). *Ten Years of Activities 1971-1981,* OAS, Washington, D.C.

JORDAN, A.M. (1978). 'Recent developments in techniques for tsetse control' in *Medical Entomological Centenary Symposium Proceedings.* Royal Society of Tropical Medicine and Hygiene, London, pp. 76-84.

KLAMARCK, M. (1976). *The Tropics and Economic Development*, Johns Hopkins University Press, Baltimore.

LAINSON, R. (1979). 'Chagas' disease in the Amazon Basin' in Trypanosoma cruzi infections in sylvatic animals, triatomine bugs and man in the State of Para, N. Brazil, *Transactions of the Royal Society of Tropical Medicine and Hygiene,* London. Vol. 73, No. 2.

LAINSON, R. (1983). 'The American Leishmaniasis: Some Observations on their Ecology and Epidemiology', *Transactions of the Royal Society of Tropical Medicine and Hygiene,* London. Vol. 77, No. 5, pp. 569-596.

LAL, R. and RUSSELL, E.W. (1981). *Tropical Agricultural Hydrology,* Wiley, pp. 131-140.

LANLY, J. (1982). *Tropical Forest Resources,* FAO Forestry Paper No. 30, Rome.

LIGHTBOURNE, R., SINGH, S. and GREEN, C. (1982). 'The World Fertility Survey: Charting Global Childbearing' in *Population Bulletin,* Vol. 37, No. 1.

LINEAR, M. (1981). 'Zapping Africa's Flies' in *Vole,* London, pp. 14-18.

MACDONALD, L. (1984). 'Wound in the World' in *Asiaweek,* 13 July 1984, Hong Kong.

MYERS, N. (1980). *Conversion of Tropical Moist Forests.* Washington, D.C., National Academy of Science.

MYERS, N. (1984). 'The Himalayas: An Influence on 500 Million People', in *Earthwatch,* No. 17, London.

MYERS N. (1979). *The Sinking Ark*, Pergamon Press, Oxford.

NASH, T.A.M. (1978). 'A review of mainly entomological research which has aided the understanding of human trypanosomiasis and its control' in *Medical Entomological Centenary Symposium Proceedings*. Royal Society of Tropical Medicine and Hygiene, London, pp. 39-47.

NATIONAL ACADEMY OF SCIENCES (1983). *Changing Climate*, National Academy Press, Washington, D.C.

O'LEARY, D.T. (1982). *Health Aspects of Watershed Development and Irrigation Projects*. World Bank, Washington, D.C., Course Note 883.

ORGANIZATION OF AMERICAN STATES (1984). Department of Regional Development, Secretariat for Economics and Social Affairs. *Integrated Regional Development Planning: Guidelines and Case-Studies from OAS Experience*, Washington, D.C.

ORMEROD, W.E. (1978). 'The relationship between economic development and ecological degradation: how degradation has occurred in West Africa and how its progress might be halted' in *Journal of Arid Environments*, Vol. 1, No. 4, London.

PARSONS, J.J. (1978). 'The changing nature of New World tropical forests since European colonization' in *The Use of Ecological Guidelines for Development in the American Humid Tropics*. IUCN publication N.S. 31, pp. 23-38.

PIMENTEL, D. (1983). 'Human populations and natural resources'. Paper prepared for Workshop on Population and Natural Resources, Cornell University, Ithaca.

PRESCOTT-ALLEN, R. & C. (1983). *Genes from the Wild,* Earthscan, London.

RAYBOULD, J.M. and WHITE, G.B. (1979). 'The distribution, bionomic and control of Onchocerciasis Vectors (Diptera: Simuliidae) in Eastern Africa and the Yemen' in *Tropenmedizin und Parasitologie,* Hamburg, Vol. 30, No. 4, pp. 409-552.

REIFSNYDER, W.E. (1982). *The Role of Forests in the Global and Regional Water and Energy Balances*, New Haven.

REIFSNYDER, W.E. (1984). 'Hydrologic Process Models'. Paper presented at UN University Workshop on Forests, Climate, Hydrology − Regional Impacts. Oxford.

REVELLE, R. (1983). 'The effects of population growth on renewable resources'. Paper presented at the International Conference on Population, Mexico City, 1984.

ROSS, M.S. and DONOVAN, D. (1984), 'Clearance of Tropical Moist Forests for Conversion to Alternative Land Uses.' International Institute for the Environment and Development, London (unpublished).

ROWNTREE, P.R. (1984). 'Review of general circulation models as a basis for predicting the effects of vegetation change on climate.' Paper presented at the UN University Workshop on Forests, Climate, Hydrology − Regional Impacts. Oxford.

SALATI, E., LOVEJOY, T.E. and VOSE, P.B. (1983). *Precipitation and Water Recycling in Tropical Rain Forests with special reference to the Amazon Basin.*

SCHOFIELD, C.J. and WHITE, G.B. (1983). 'Engineering against insect-borne diseases in the domestic environment: House design and domestic vectors of disease' in *Transactions of the Royal Society of Tropical Medicine and Hygiene,* London, Vol. 78, pp. 285-292.

SCOTT, G.L. (1979). 'Recognising the "invisible" woman in development' in *The World Bank's Experience* World Bank, Washington, D.C.

SECLA, (1983). 'Development, life styles, population and environment in Latin America'. Paper presented at the International Conference on Population, Mexico City, 1984.

SHIKLOMANOV, I.A. and KRESTOVYKS, O.I. (1984). 'The influence of forests and forest reclamation practice on stream flow and water balance'. Paper presented at the UN University Workshop on Forests, Climate, Hydrology — Regional Impacts, Oxford.

SMITH, N.J.H. (1981). 'Colonisation Lessons from a Tropical Forest' in *Science*, Vol. 214, pp. 755-760.

SPEARS, J. (1983). *Sustainable Land Use and Strategy Options for Management and Conservation of the Moist Tropical Forest Eco-system.* International Symposium on Tropical Deforestation, Wageningen.

SPEARS, J. (1983). *Saving the Tropical Forest Ecosytem — A Discussion Paper*, World Bank, Washington, D.C.

TOLBA, M.U. (1982). *Development without Destruction: Evolving Environmental Perceptions*, Tycooly Institute, Dublin.

U.N. (1980). *Patterns of Urban and Rural Population Growth.* Population Study No. 68, New York.

U.S. DEPARTMENT OF STATE (1982). *Proceedings on the U.S. Strategy Conference on Biological Diversity.*

WALLACE, M.B. (1982). *Solving Common Property Resource Problems: Deforestation in Nepal* (thesis), Harvard University, Cambridge, Mass.

WORLD BANK. (1984). *World Development Report.* New York and Oxford. Oxford University Press.

Appendix: Information Note on the Independent Commission on International Humanitarian Issues

The establishment of an Independent Commission on International Humanitarian Issues is the response of a group of eminent persons from all parts of the world to the deeply felt need to enhance public awareness of important humanitarian issues and to promote an international climate favouring progress in the humanitarian field.

The work of the Commission is intended to be a part of the continuing search of the world community for a more adequate international framework to uphold human dignity and rise to the challenge of colossal humanitarian problems arising with increasing frequency in all continents.

In 1981, the UN General Assembly adopted by consensus a resolution relating to a 'new international humanitarian order' in which it recognized: 'the importance of further improving a comprehensive international framework which takes fully into account existing instruments relating to humanitarian questions as well as the need for addressing those aspects which are not yet adequately covered'. In doing so, the Assembly bore in mind that 'institutional arrangements and actions of governmental and non-governmental bodies might need to be further strengthened to respond effectively in situations requiring humanitarian action.'

The following year, the General Assembly adopted by consensus a further resolution relating to the International Humanitarian Order noting 'the proposal for establishment, outside the United Nations framework, of an "Independent Commission on International Humanitarian Issues" composed of leading personalities in the humanitarian field or having wide experience of government or world affairs.'

The Independent Commission on International Humanitarian Issues was inaugurated in July 1983 and held its first plenary meeting in New York in November 1983. A few days later, the UN General Assembly adopted another resolution in which it noted the establishment of the Commission and requested the Secretary-General to remain in contact with governments as well as with the Independent Commission in order to provide a comprehensive report on the humanitarian order to the Assembly.

In 1985, the United Nations Secretary-General presented to the General Assembly a comprehensive report and comments from governments on the 'new international humanitarian order'. The report included a description of the Independent Commission and its work. In a subsequent resolution adopted by consensus, the General Assembly took note of the activities of the Commission and looked forward to the outcome of its efforts and its Final Report.

Composition of the Commission

The Commission is an independent body whose members participate in their personal capacity and not as representatives of governments or international bodies to which they may belong. Its work is not intended to interfere with governmental negotiations or inter-state relations nor to duplicate work being done by existing governmental or non-governmental bodies.

In its deliberations, the Commission benefits from the advice of governments, existing international governmental and non-governmental bodies and leading experts. The Commission operates through a small Secretariat which coordinates research activities and provides support services for the work of the Commission. The composition of the Commission, which is intended to remain limited, is based on equitable geographical distribution. At present, it has twenty-seven members.

Programme of Work

In the course of its limited life span of three years, 1983-1986, the Commission has dealt with a wide range of subjects relating to humanitarian issues of relevance to contemporary society. The main areas which have been selected by the Independent Commission for study are:

(i)   Humanitarian norms in the context of armed conflicts.
(ii)   Natural and man-made disasters.
(iii) Vulnerable groups requiring special care and protection such as refugees and displaced persons, stateless persons, children and youth, indigenous populations, etc.

The conclusions and recommendations of the Commission will be based on in-depth studies of selected subjects carried out with the help of recognized experts and national or international bodies chosen from all parts of the world for their specialized knowledge or experience. In addition to direct input by experts in the form of policy-orientated research papers, the Commission also sponsors panel discussions or brainstorming sessions. Similarly, close contact is maintained with agencies dealing with subjects of interest to the Commission in order to avoid duplication of effort, complement ongoing projects and exercise a catalytic influence in promoting innovative solutions. Heads of these agencies or their representatives are invited to testify at the Commission's bi-annual plenary sessions.

The in-depth studies and expert advice received by the Commission have been instrumental in the preparation of sectoral reports on particular humanitarian issues which are published for public distribution in order to encourage timely follow-up action. The sectoral reports are addressed to policy-makers within governments, regional bodies, inter-governmental and private voluntary agencies and the general public.

The first sectoral report entitled *Famine: A Man-Made Disaster?* was published in 1985. The purpose of this report is to increase public awareness of the famine conditions afflicting much of Africa and the Third World, recommend positive solutions and facilitate further study and analysis of the situation. The report has already been published in eight languages.

Sectoral reports on deforestation (the present report) and desertification as well as street children were published early in 1986. Additional reports on disappeared persons, humanitarian norms in armed conflict, refugees and other humanitarian topics are forthcoming.

The overall efforts of the Commission are thus a pyramid-like process which will culminate in the preparation of its Final Report scheduled for the end of 1986. The Final Report will address the humanitarian implications of a diverse range of global issues and set forth a viable framework for the implementation of a new international humanitarian order. It will be a policy and practice-oriented blueprint for effective response to the colossal challenge posed by humanitarian problems.

Members of the Commission

Sadruddin AGA KHAN (Iran) – UN High Commissioner for Refugees, 1965-77. Special Consultant to the UN Secretary-General since 1978. Special Rapporteur of the UN Human Rights Commission, 1981. Founder-President of the Bellerive Group.

Susanna AGNELLI (Italy) — Under-Secretary of State for Foreign Affairs since 1983. Member of the Italian Senate. Member of the European Parliament, 1979-81. Journalist and author.

Talal Bin Abdul Aziz AL SAUD (Saudi Arabia) — President, the Arab Gulf Programme for UN Development Organizations (AGFUND). UNICEF's Special Envoy, 1980-84. Former Administrator of Royal Palaces, Minister of Communications, of Finance and National Economy, and Vice-President of the Supreme Planning Commission.

Paulo Evaristo ARNS (Brazil) — Cardinal Archbishop of Sao Paulo. Chancellor of the Pontifical Catholic University, Sao Paulo State. Author.

Mohammed BEDJAOUI (Algeria) — Judge at the International Court of Justice since 1982. Secretary-General, Council of Ministers, 1962-64; Minister of Justice, 1964-70. Ambassador to France, 1970-79; UNESCO, 1971-79; and the United Nations in New York, 1979-82.

Henrik BEER (Sweden) — Secretary-General of the League of Red Cross Societies, 1960-82. Secretary-General of the Swedish Red Cross. 1947-60. Member of the International Institute for Environment and Development and the International Institute of Humanitarian Law.

Luis ECHEVERRIA ALVAREZ (Mexico) — President of the Republic, 1970-76; Founder and Director-General of the Centre for Economic and Social Studies of the Third World since 1976. Former Ambassador to Australia, New Zealand and UNESCO.

Pierre GRABER (Switzerland) — President of the Swiss Confederation, 1975. Foreign Minister, 1975-78. President of the Diplomatic Conference on Humanitarian Law, 1974-77.

Ivan L. HEAD (Canada) — President of the International Development Research Centre (IDRC). Special Assistant to the Prime Minister of Canada, 1968-78. Queen's Counsel.

M. HIDAYATULLAH (India) — Vice-President of India, 1979-84. Chief Justice of the Supreme Court, 1968-70; Chief Justice of the Nagpur and Madhya Pradesh High Courts, 1954-58; Chancellor of the Jamia Millia Islamia since 1979. Former Chancellor of the Universities of Delhi, Punjab. Author.

Aziza HUSSEIN (Egypt) — Member of the Population Council. President of the International Planned Parenthood Federation, 1977-85. Fellow at the International Peace Academy, Helsinki, 1971; the Aspen Institute of Humanistic Studies, 1978-79.

Manfred LACHS (Poland) — Judge at the International Court of Justice since 1967 and its President, 1973-76. Professor of Political Science and International Law. Former Chairman of the UN Legal Committee on the Peaceful Uses of Outer Space.

Robert S. McNAMARA (USA) — President of the World Bank, 1968-81; Secretary of Defense, 1961-68. President, Ford Motor Company, 1960-61. Trustee of the Brookings Institute, Ford Foundation, the Urban Institute and the California Institute of Technology. Author.

Lazar MOJSOV (Yugoslavia) — Member of the Presidency of the Socialist Federal Republic of Yugoslavia. Former Foreign Minister. Ambassador to the USSR, Mongolia, Austria, the United Nations, 1958-74. President of the UN General Assembly, 32nd Session and of the Special Session on Disarmament, 1978.

Mohamed MZALI (Tunisia) — Prime Minister and General Secretary of the Destorian Socialist Party. Member of the National Assembly since 1959. Former Minister of National Defence, Education, Youth and Sports and Health. Author.

Sadako OGATA (Japan) — Professor at the Institute of International Relations, Sophia University, Tokyo. Representative of Japan to the United Nations Human Rights Commission. Member of the Trilateral Commission.

David OWEN (United Kingdom) — Member of Parliament since 1966. Leader of the Social Democratic Party since 1983. Foreign Secretary, 1977-79.

Willibald P. PAHR (Austria) — Secretary-General of the World Tourism Organization. Federal Minister of Foreign Affairs, 1976-83. Ambassador. Vice-President of the International Institute of Human Rights (Strasbourg).

Shridath S. RAMPHAL (Guyana) — Secretary-General of the Commonwealth since 1975. Former Attorney-General, Foreign Minister and Minister of Justice.

RU XIN (China) — Vice-President of the Chinese Academy of Social Sciences. Professor of Philosophy at the Xiamen University. Executive President of the Chinese National Society of the History of World Philosophies.

Salim A. SALIM (Tanzania) — Deputy Prime Minister and Minister of Defence. Former Prime Minister and Foreign Minister. Ambassador to Egypt, India, China and Permanent Representative to the United Nations. Former President of the UN General Assembly and the Security Council.

Léopold Sédar SENGHOR (Senegal) — Member of the French Academy. President of the Republic of Senegal, 1960-80. Cabinet Minister in the French Government before leading his country to independence in 1960. Poet and philosopher.

SOEDJATMOKO (Indonesia) — Rector of the United Nations University, Tokyo, since 1980. Ambassador to the United States. Member of the Club of Rome and Trustee of the Aspen Institute and the Ford Foundation.

Hassan bin TALAL (Jordan) — Crown Prince of the Hashemite Kingdom. Founder of the Royal Scientific Society and the Arab Thought Forum. Concerned with development planning and the formulation of national, economic and social policies. Author.

Desmond TUTU (South Africa) — Archbishop of Cape Town. Winner of Nobel Peace Prize. Former Secretary-General of the South African Council of Churches. Professor of Theology.

Simone VEIL (France) — Member of the European Parliament and its President 1979-82; chairs the Legal Affairs Committee of the European Parliament. Former Minister of Health, Social Security and Family Affairs, 1974-79.

E. Gough WHITLAM (Australia) — Prime Minister, 1972-75; Minister of Foreign Affairs, 1972-73; Member of Parliament, 1952-78. Ambassador to UNESCO.

Titles on the Environment

Bina Agarwal
COLD HEARTHS AND BARREN SLOPES
The Woodfuel Crisis in the Third World
1986

Clyde Sanger
ORDERING THE OCEANS
The Making of the Law of the Sea
1986

*A Report for the Independent Commission on
International Humanitarian Issues*
THE VANISHING FOREST
The Human Consequences of Deforestation
1986

*A Report for the Independent Commission on
International Humanitarian Issues*
THE ENCROACHING DESERT
The Consequences of Human Failure
1986

Sue Branford and Oriel Glock
THE LAST FRONTIER
Fighting over Land in the Amazon
1985

Ted Trainer
ABANDON AFFLUENCE!
1985

Vaclav Smil
THE BAD EARTH
Environmental Degradation in China
1984

The above titles are available in both a cased and limp
edition, and can be ordered direct from Zed Books Ltd.,
57 Caledonian Road, London N1 9BU. If you are
interested in a full Catalogue of Zed titles on the Third
World, please write to the same address.